The Henderson County Curb Market

A Blue Ridge Heritage
Since 1924

By

Ann Greenleaf Wirtz

2010
Parkway Publishers, Inc.
Boone, North Carolina

© 2010 by Ann Greenleaf Wirtz
All Rights Reserved

Library of Congress Cataloging-in-Publication Data

Wirtz, Ann Greenleaf.
 The Henderson County Curb Market : a Blue Ridge heritage since 1924 / by Ann Greenleaf Wirtz
       p. cm.
  ISBN 978-1-933251-71-4
  1. Curb Market (Henderson County, N.C.)--History. 2. Farmers' markets--North Carolina--Henderson County--History. I. Title.
   HF5472.U7H469 2010
   381'.41--dc22
                              2010013554

Parkway Publishers, Inc.
PO Box 3678
Boone, North Carolina 28607
Ph. & Fax.: (828) 265-3993
www.parkwaypublishers.com

Dedicated
to the
Curb Market
Founding Families
and to
Devoted Members,
past and present.

Your hard work and creativity
are forever
satisfying, wholesome,
and
inspirational.

Acknowledgments

As nearly two and a half years of research and interviews come to a close, I'm pleased to acknowledge those who were so helpful in providing valuable information and support for this book:

Pat Walker was nearby when the idea first came to mind and happily answered some of my immediate questions about the Curb Market. She's been nearby ever since with encouragement, insight, and the willingness to lend me the treasured Curb scrapbooks so indispensible to this account.

Vena Robinson was Pat Walker's aunt, and she could well be considered the historian of the Curb Market in light of her commitment to compiling these scrapbooks. She included newspaper articles, pictures, and personal writings given to her by other members, or through her own discovery, that tell both the Curb's history and the Market's unfolding events. Vena preserved the Curb Market record, and she is owed an enormous debt of gratitude.

Terry Robinson is Vena's son, and he and Pat Walker provided an invaluable service to the Curb Market in 1999 when they compiled *Members of the Henderson County Curb Market, 75 years of memories*. Their booklet presents pictures and brief memoirs that define the Curb's story. It would have been impossible to write *The Henderson County Curb Market, A Blue Ridge Heritage* without their "book of memories."

Nancy Ball was another invaluable resource for stories, insight and inspiration.

Ralph King provided gentle wisdom and guidance that clarified the historic roots of the Market.

Elaine Staton always had answers for my questions and a smile for my efforts.

Vendors, customers, and individuals in the community gave legs to this book through their memorable Curb Market narratives.

Members of the Henderson County Genealogical and Historical Society have been supportive of this endeavor and extremely helpful in uncovering maternal family lines. Maiden names are important to the Curb's historical record, as Market tables have often been acquired through a mother's lineage. Recognizing both sides of the Curb's family tree has been an important goal.

My appreciation goes to Jeannie Lindsey, Ginny Thompson and others from the Historical Society who helped me with this specific research. Thanks also to Dr. George A. and Evelyn Jones and Alexia Jones Helsley for their friendship and personal encouragement.

And to my treasured friends and family, gratitude and love for your prayerful support, especially my Dearest Ones:

Arie Todd and Dewa Shrestha Greenleaf, my wonderful son and his precious wife, parents of my beautiful granddaughter, Divya;

Jack and Helen Patrick Wirtz, my loving parents;

W. Patrick Wirtz, my forever amazing and adored husband, who helped with all aspects of the computer, and who's been behind me every step of the way.

Thank you!

Table of Contents

The Artist ~ Carolyn DeMorest Serrano ~ xi

How This Book Came to Be ~ Ann Brubaker Greenleaf Wirtz ~ xiii

"Our Curb Market" ~ Poem by Grace Johnson Holleman ~ xvi

1. A Walk Down the Aisles 1
2. In the Beginning..5
3. Pioneer Families..13
4. From Under the Umbrellas...19
5. Memories from Golden Glow Farm ~ Frank L. FitzSimons Jr. & III 25
6. Managing the Market ~ French and Bobbi Hill Rogers 31
7. The Storybook Dolls Lady ~ Ersie Griffin Ratliff Davis..................35
8. Maintaining the Flow ~ Stanley and Elaine Duncan Staton.................39
9. Flowers: Dried, Arranged, Inviting ~ Larry and Nancy Justice Ball.......43
10. The Wildflower Lady and Her Cousins ~ Louise Jackson Hill & the Kings....47
11. From the Beginning ~ Pat Walker..53
12. World-renowned Artist and Author ~ RuthEllen Connell Boerman 57
13. Pickles and Chutney ~ Joyce Hill Pace 61
14. Angels, Bonnets, Caramel Cake, and Dolls ~ Marilyn Pryor Horne.........65
15. Recipes for Life and Homemade Bread ~ Ruby Jones King 71
16. A Way of Life ~ Mary Staton Jones......................................77
17. Lining up for Iris, Peaches, Apples and Plants ~ Russell Lyda..........81
18. Oh, Those Deviled Eggs ~ Earl and Fran Hudson Griffin 85
19. Venetian Art Glass and Sourdough Bread ~ The Dolan Family..............89
20. Rustic Creativity ~ Donald and Doris Dill Moore 93
21. A Family Tradition ~ Freddie and Phyllis Ruff Rhodes 97
22. The Toy Maker of the Curb Market ~ Velton A. Searcy...................103
23. Curb Connections ~ The Hyder, Lyda, Gilbert Families 109
24. Fried Apple Pies ~ Dorothy Clingenpeel Barnwell.......................113
25. A Treasured Heritage ~ Thomas and Jane Duncan Henderson 117
26. Log Cabin Woodworks ~ David Taylor....................................123

27. A Mother and Daughter ~ Ida Barnwell Freeman & Liz Enloe 127
28. Memories to Share ~ Kenneth G. Justus 131
29. The Nicest People ~ Thomas B. Corbett 135
30. An Entrepreneurial Spirit ~ Linda Lytle Justice 139
31. A Mountain Story ~ Christine Williams Jackson 143
32. Knowing the Ones Who Grow Our Food ~ Williams, Nix, Capps 147
33. Two We Can't Forget ~ Hoyte Kerr Jones & Hazel Whittington 151
34. In Conclusion ~ The Clyde and Sarah Maude Ramsey Pace Family 155
35. The "Book of Memories" 159

Appendices:
Articles from The Hendersonville News and The Times-News 163
Calendars 168
Family Names of Current & Former Stock Holders and/or Vendors 169
Notes 171

The Artist
Carolyn DeMorest Serrano
A Pen and Ink Drawing of the Curb Market

Photo by Ann Wirtz

An intricate drawing of today's Curb Market graces the cover of this book, a pen and ink rendering by artist Carolyn DeMorest Serrano. As a vendor at the Curb since Labor Day weekend, 2005, Carolyn knows the spirit and creativity of the Market first hand.

Originally from the Lansing, Michigan area, Carolyn moved to Hendersonville in 1994 from Houston, Texas. She brought an amazing talent and commitment to preserving local history through her artwork, which encompasses everything from antique tractors and automobiles to well-known buildings that symbolize and identify a community. She has drawn the Old Federal Building on the corner of 4th Avenue and Church Street, where she maintains an art space to compliment her days at the Curb Market.

Familiar landmarks like the Historic Henderson County Courthouse, the

Seventh Avenue Railroad Depot, and the old Hooper's Creek Grocery are part of Carolyn's wide-ranging portfolio. Her artwork includes country churches and the First Baptist Church in downtown Hendersonville. She is regularly commissioned to draw both private and historic homes, such as the Smith-McDowell House in Asheville.

Carolyn is in the memory business. "There's a pull on the heartstrings," is the way she describes the emotional response to her drawings, which call forth the memories people have concerning her work.

She has a dual sensitivity to design and human interest. These combine with her skills and find expression through the tools of her trade: a camera for original photos, black technical pens with the finest of tips, a ruler, and mechanical pencils. Sketched on heavy 100-pound illustration board, each drawing takes an average of 50 hours to complete. Many times her picture shows two or three different perspectives of the subject.

In September, 2004, Carolyn began working with the Henderson County Education Foundation on a fundraiser to present a pen and ink collection of all 13 Henderson County schools. Her work now completed, her drawings provide an historical record of the schools treasured by students, teachers and administrators alike. Eight by ten inch prints along with note cards can be purchased of each school campus.

For over ten years, Carolyn has been a member of the Heritage Crafters. This group displays their arts and crafts as well as demonstrates their talents at the North Carolina Mountain State Fair every September at the Agricultural Center in Fletcher. Since 2006, she has been part of the Village of Yesteryear at the North Carolina State Fair in Raleigh.

Carolyn and her husband, Ed, are members of the First Baptist Church in Hendersonville, where she teaches the Special Friends Sunday School Class for special-needs adults. She's also on the Mayor's Committee for People with Disabilities. Throughout the month, Carolyn can be found teaching a seniors' drawing class at various assisted-living centers. She holds classes at the summer art camp for children at historic Johnson Farm and demonstrates her talent at special events held there.

Active, committed, talented, and faithful to the Lord are words that best describe the essence of Carolyn DeMorest Serrano.

How This Book Came to Be
Ann Brubaker Greenleaf Wirtz

Ann Greenleaf Wirtz
Chuck Hill Photography

There've been Brubakers in the Blue Ridge since at least 1789. The family originated in Switzerland, but my fourth great-grandfather, John, came from Germany, where Brubakers fled as early as 1527 to escape religious persecution. (1) After coming to America, John married Anna Myers. This family eventually left Lancaster County, Pennsylvania, and traveled south on The Great Philadelphia Wagon Road with their six children, Henry being the oldest. They settled on land in Franklin County then Roanoke County, Virginia. Joel was son to Henry, and Noah was born in 1836 to Joel and Elizabeth Fisher Brubaker. As a young man, Noah headed to Ohio, where he married and was widowed. He and his second wife, Elizabeth Baird, continued westward, living throughout various mid-western states. In 1900, they established a final residence in Sawyer, Kansas, and two years later an Old German Baptist Brethren Church. Noah became one of two ordained Elders to preach and guide the Sawyer congregation. He and Elizabeth are my great-grandparents, and still flourishing today are the farms and families of dear Brubaker cousins, members of this Plain, Anabaptist denomination, still worshiping in the original, yet simply remodeled church. Kansas was home to my parents, Kenneth and Charlotte Remick Brubaker, and I was born in Wichita.

The lovely Blue Ridge of North Carolina, just south of the Brubaker homesteads in the mountains of Virginia, became my home in 2002. My late first husband, Arie Greenleaf, and I were drawn to the beauty of Henderson County, as so many are today. Living on top of Davis Mountain provided the vistas and natural habitat that thrilled our mid-western hearts. Still, aware of my Blue Ridge heritage, I knew a sense of belonging.

Following my husband's unexpected cancer diagnosis and death in 2004, prayer and patience brought the direction to begin writing, a long-held dream I was thrilled to explore. There was great joy in this pastime; I considered writing the happiest thing I did while coping with the loneliness of widowhood. Writing the story of God's faithfulness as we dealt with cancer was very therapeutic and led to my book on loss and grief, *Sorrow Answered*.

In the final month of Arie's life, I received a clear answer from the Lord about my future: I was to go forward unafraid, trusting in Him. That first difficult Sunday after my husband's death, a friend observed my loneliness and suggested I join the choir. I sensed this was to be part of my "going forward" and joined the next rehearsal.

Patrick Wirtz was the choir director, a Hendersonville native, a casual friend who came with our pastor to visit us during Arie's illness...and he was single...and he was cute. Not that I ever thought much about that, honestly, knowing I was some older than he is. But thankfully, God has plans for us, usually beyond our imagining, and after that first year of widowhood, both Patrick and I began to see the possibility of a future together. Indeed, we were married April 21, 2006, and wedded joy has been our companion ever since.

By this time, I had written a few articles which, surprising to this new writer, were published in the Times-News. A few months later, I was asked to write regularly for the Crossroads section of the paper. It was a wonderful opportunity to meet fascinating people and to learn about important community ministries. I was grateful to continue writing, one of my most satisfying and meaningful activities.

A year later on an October Saturday, 2007, I held a book signing at the Curb Market. I brought copies of *Sorrow Answered* and sold more than I ever anticipated. During a lull, I was contemplating my next book, praying for inspiration, actually, when what I've come to recognize as the Lord's clear direction entered my heart and mind: Write the history of the Curb Market.

I was astonished, to say the least, but mostly I was excited by the possibility. I loved visiting the Curb, always admiring the vendors and their talents and livelihood on display, but perhaps a book had already been written? I asked around and, "No," there existed only chapters about the Market, primarily the chapter in Frank L. FitzSimons' book, *From The Banks of The Oklawaha, Volume II*.

And so, the adventure began. I've been both humbled and honored to write this book, considering it a great privilege. As I've researched, interviewed and written the story of the Curb Market, I've covered the history and the highlights of this county gem as best I could, ever aware the sheer volume of people, memories, and stories would sadly make it impossible to include all. The lists of stockholders and vendors in Chapter 35 and the Appendix, while incomplete, are my way of including "everyone."

Over these past two and a half years, I've come to know and deeply appreciate the people, those today and those long gone, who made and now make the Curb possible. This is a remarkable local treasure, one that needs to be better understood for what it represents about Henderson County. It is history, alive and frankly in want of greater support as the ol' time generations pass away and knowledge about the Market fades before new generations and those recent to the community.

The first verse in a poem about my great-grandfather Noah recognizes that memories keep alive the story of our lives. I see the Curb Market in this context, with the journeys of the earliest members ended, but their accomplishments still with us and waiting to be shared...with the stories and memories of those at the Curb today important to its history. The poem begins:

From the mountains of Virginia
To the sunbathed western plain;
Grandpa's journey now has ended,
But his mem'ries still remain.

Dear Reader, as we explore the history and memories that still remain about this special place, my hopes for you are simply: for my penned experiences to be yours...for my memories to kindle your own...for my Curb purchases to be ones you desire...and for my visits and support of this enterprising place to inspire your own personal commitment to the Curb Market.

Blessings,
Ann Brubaker Greenleaf Wirtz
January 4, 2010
Hendersonville, North Carolina

Our Curb Market

By Mrs. Harvey Holleman
(Grace Johnson McGuire Holleman)

Each week it is my pleasure,
As Saturdays come and go,
To stroll through the Curb Market
And greet the friends I know.
There are many tempting cakes
And jellies and jams,
And sorghum and stacks of yams,
And the friendly sausage man,
Selling his pork and hams.
There are chickens, rabbits,
Cracklings and cottage cheese
homemade,
There's popcorn and walnuts,
And cut flowers of every shade,
Hand crafts and rugs,
Handbags and aprons gay,
Cider to refresh you,
And apples to store away.
And 'long about the Yuletide,
There's holly and galax leaves,
Wreathes of cones and seed,
Decorations for every need.
There's Mrs. Coston, the manager,
To hand out change and cheer
And there's Fred Nix and directors,
Always standing near.
It's a show place 'n our city,
An old-time rendezvous,
Yet, as often as I go there,
There's always something new!

Chapter One
A Walk Down the Aisles

A Colorful Booth, Dorothy Barnwell
(Photo by Ann Wirtz)

A unique combination of personal independence, creativity, and accomplishment resides at the heart of the American narrative. A devotion to God nurtures the soul of our nation's story, from the Pilgrims' prayerful voyage to our religious freedom today. A rhythm as ancient as time underlies the farmer's seasonal commitment to till, plant, and harvest the land's bounty, ever the thread of life's sustaining nourishment.

Nowhere are these features: the American spirit, the heritage of faith, and the pattern of life more evident and intertwined than in a country market. In historic Hendersonville, North Carolina, these attributes are found in the Henderson County Farmers Mutual Curb Market, simply known as the Curb Market, at 221 North Church Street.

The essence of America's best is found in a walk down the Curb's colorful aisles, with each booth representing an historical past, a lively present, and a hope for the future. The history of the Henderson County Curb Market dates back informally to 1922 when a letter was written by Frank L. FitzSimons and sent to the local newspaper to propose what he called *"a central marketing place...along a street called a curb market."* (1) It took several years to gather support and work through the challenges, but farm families came together to start the Curb Market in 1924 with the help of FitzSimons and Noah Hollowell, editor and publisher of that local newspaper, The Hendersonville News.

From these roots, today's Curb Market continues the heritage of Appalachian Mountain industry and hard work. The present is a fascinating array of human endeavor sufficient to make the old-timers proud.

A current brochure touts:
Freshly Baked: Cakes, Pies, Candies, Jams & Jellies;
Hand Made: Artistic Woodwork, Soaps, Toys, Linens, Rugs & Wreaths;
Home Grown: Fruits, Vegetables, Cut Flowers & Plants.

The result is:
in many a local and distant home there may be found...
farm fresh produce for the evening meal,
a painted, wooden Noah's Ark puzzle,
an old-fashioned, hand-woven rug,
a delicately embroidered table runner or towel,
a one-of-a-kind necklace,
a festive apron,
a gorgeous, dried flower arrangement,
handcrafted or sewn toys and dolls,
soy candles and goat cheese,
plaques and wooden designs,
pen and ink drawings or colorful paintings,
Sara Edney's cleverly painted gourds,
pure sourwood honey and molasses,
rich, blackberry jelly,
a jar of delicious dill pickles,
and in the fall...
a traditional bittersweet bouquet
along with juicy apples
fresh from the nearby orchards.

And if one is very fortunate,
at any time of the year,
a Marilyn Horne, to-die-for Caramel Cake!

Crocheted and knitted afghans and quilts reside alongside homemade breads and desserts, jars of pickled okra and beans, garden plants and vegetables, all exciting the imagination with decorating and landscaping schemes and the anticipation of delectable food. It's a feast for the eyes and a balm to the soul to see such goodness on display. It's actually a momentary escape into a world where thoughtful ingenuity meets delightful talent, and one is in awe of the resourcefulness of the people.

Ah, the people. Behind each booth sits those who are devoted to preserving the creative strength of the Curb Market. And in them, and others like them, is our future hope: that the continuation of personal integrity and industry will forever be the heartbeat of our nation.

These very attributes course through the history of the Curb Market as it unfolds through the stories of its vendors. From the earliest written records to the memories and thoughts of second, third, fourth-generation sellers still maintaining or contributing to a booth today, the stories reveal an inspiring work ethic and continuity of purpose. The *"oldest and most successful farmer's cooperative effort in Henderson County,"* as the Curb was described by Frank L. FitzSimons in Volume II of his book, *From The Banks of The Oklawaha,* (2) is a community treasure worth celebrating.

Since families are the key to the Market's success, the Appendix provides an incomplete list of the surnames of former and current Curb Market members dating back to 1924. It's understood that many individuals, too numerous to record, will be represented by each single family name. A list of specific stock holders and vendors identified in the 1999 booklet, *Members of the Henderson County Curb Market, 75 years of memories* is found in Chapter 35, as these individuals and families are a bridge to the past.

With each passing year, every accolade and honor given and still to be received by the Curb Market is highly deserved. This business model has given the people of Henderson County a financial resource, food, friendship, beauty, and a glimpse into the tenacity of the human spirit. Farm families started the market, and while farms are fewer in number than ever before, and unfortunately getting fewer, a patch of soil and an industrious soul can still grow flowers and vegetables to sell, plant orchards to share fruit in abundance, make jams and jellies from the harvested bounty, and keep alive that rhythm of life that sustains us.

Change is inevitable and sometimes beneficial, but there's a nostalgic romance and truth that will always be associated with the traditional, timeless, simply unchanging, God-given basics of life: faith, love, garden fare, and the soul's desire for creative expression. Somehow, all this gets wrapped-up in a stroll through a farmer's market.

Going down the aisles of the Henderson County Curb Market and relishing the productivity of the vendors who make this place so distinctive is a treat for both soul and senses alike. Thus the story unfolds, and it's a good one.

Chapter Two
In the Beginning

F.L. FitzSimons
(Photo courtesy of The Hendersonville News, August 4, 1925)

Noah Hollowell
(Photo courtesy of the Curb Market)

Frank Lockwood FitzSimons Sr...

known for residing
at Golden Glow Farm in Dana
where he and his wife, Maggie,
had a dairy farm and apple orchard,
was a Marine Corpsman
and winner of the Navy Cross for valor during World War I,
was a teacher for 20 years,
was twice elected to the office of the Register of Deeds,
was a bank Vice President
and on the Board of Directors during his 25 years in banking,
was a beloved WHKP radio broadcaster for 25 years,
was a noted author
with excerpts from over 5,000 of his radio programs
the genesis of his award-winning books,
the three-volume series about Henderson County,
From The Banks of The Oklawaha...
is considered the Curb Market's inspirational founder.

FitzSimons himself penned a chapter on the Curb Market's historic beginning in Volume II of his trilogy. He describes his 1922 letter to the editor in which he proposes the formation of a local farmers' market similar to the open air markets he saw in Europe during World War I. A local resident following the war, FitzSimons moved here in 1920 to accept a teaching position at Hendersonville High School. Originally from Grand Rapids, Michigan, where he was born in 1897, FitzSimons grew up in Spartanburg, South Carolina and spent his early summers in Henderson County. His letter to Noah Hollowell of The Hendersonville News presented an idea that dovetailed with Hollowell's own desire for the development and advancement of the county's agricultural resources.

An article appears on the front page of the "News," as the paper was commonly called, providing insight into this young veteran's relationship with the community. Published on Friday, February 24, 1922, the article is titled *"F. L. FitzSimons Leases Dairy Farm Near City."* The story reads, *"F. L. FitzSimons, athletic manager at the city high school, has leased and moved to a 35-acre dairy farm on the Crab Creek road, which he has named the 'Golden Glow Farm.' The farm is stocked with fifteen cows and a fully equipped sanitary barn, with concrete arrangements and electric lights, and he proposes to furnish Hendersonville and surrounding community with the purest and most sanitary milk. Until he is free from his duties at the city high school the work will be carried on largely by help which he has secured. Mr. FitzSimons is well experienced in dairy work, having spent much time before he came to Hendersonville on Maryland farms which furnished Washington city with milk.*

"Mr. FitzSimons is so well pleased with Hendersonville that he contemplates permanent residence here or in this county."

According to court house records, his lease lasted two years until early 1924, when he bought 104 acres on Howard Gap Road in Dana and moved Golden Glow Farm to its beautiful new location, FitzSimons' home until his death in 1980. The distant Blue Ridge Mountains that encompass his property were to provide a serene backdrop to the active, generous life he lived in Henderson County, with the founding of the Curb Market one of his most enduring achievements. FitzSimons believed a centralized, easily accessible location for farmers to sell their produce and industry was a business model that would work in Western North Carolina.

In a speech FitzSimons presented on the Curb Market's Fiftieth Anniversary Celebration, reprinted and given to the Curb Market by FitzSimons' family, he describes a major obstacle for farmers in the early 1920s. *"Half a century or more ago growing vegetables for the market was not the multimillion dollar industry that it is today in Henderson County. Farmers who raised perishable vegetables or 'truck crops' had only a limited market."*

FitzSimons proposed his solution, one that would also provide an alternative to the wearisome routine of peddling, the standard practice of that era. Going door-to-door with baskets of items in hand was a cumbersome task. In his Fiftieth Anniversary speech, FitzSimons recalls the rigors of peddling. He said, *"Several times a week, if a farmer did not live too far from Hendersonville, he would bring his vegetables to town in buggies, wagons and occasionally in a Model T Ford. The farmer would drive up and down the streets of Hendersonville, knocking on doors of the homes, the boarding houses and hotels. With the help of an energetic wife who brought along butter, eggs, dressed and live chickens, buttermilk and sweet milk, a farmer could work both sides of a street at the same time. It was a slow, tiresome, difficult and time-consuming way to market produce. It was called 'peddling' in those days. Competition was keen and I have seen ten or twelve wagons, buggies, carts pulled by mules, horses and even here and there an ox, all within two or three blocks, peddling more or less the same things. At the end of the day, if a farmer had any unsold produce, he would stop at the grocery store and trade what he had left for coffee, tea, sugar or other needed groceries."*

As FitzSimons was formulating his curb market plans, Noah Hollowell was also considering the needs of both farmer and community. Originally from Eastern North Carolina, Hollowell came to Hendersonville in 1904 and started The News Print Shop, which is now the Flanagan Printing Company on W. 3rd Avenue. Hollowell sold it to George Flanagan and C. W. Davis, who later sold his interest to George's brother, Harold. (1)

Prior to 1922, Hollowell became the publisher and editor of The Hendersonville News. Under his leadership, the News merged with The Hendersonville Times in 1927 and became The Times-News (simply Times-News today). Since Hollowell recognized the interdependency of the farmer and the local community, he got behind the curb market concept. His support was invaluable to FitzSimons, who later wrote, "(The Curb Market) *is above all a memorial to Noah Hollowell, a great newspaper publisher, civic and religious leader."* (2)

Hollowell held many leadership positions in Henderson County, identified in a June 28, 1978 article from The Times-News titled, "Curb Market Reflects Agricultural Growth." The style of writing points to the editor Mead Parce as the unnamed author. The writer recognizes Hollowell as the former publisher-editor of The Hendersonville News, a bank president, the Chamber of Commerce secretary-manager, and the welfare official during the Depression. FitzSimons and Hollowell are lauded as co-founders of the Curb Market, "(They) *may undoubtedly be described as co-fathers (if a word coinage may be permitted) of this enterprise."*

In an editorial on Tuesday, April 25, 1922, Hollowell advocates for a centralized marketing location. He wrote, *"Garden seeds are telling their story. The next chapter will be fresh vegetables and the seeking of markets. Hendersonville is working on the market problem...Selling the idea is the main expense. For a try-out use the curb or some little designated spot. If the idea is popular enlarge on it to meet the demands.*

"We have little at stake to begin with so let's go. Designate some spot the farmer can use unmolested. Let the housewives know where he can be found, and when. Let the regulations and restrictions be few and simple and let's have the open market by the time the first vegetables are ready to market."

It usually takes time to sell an idea, and selling the curb market concept was no exception. A new idea often meets with opposition, which this proposal did. Nevertheless, interested farmers met and devised plans which were eventually presented to the mayor and city commissioners. A prominent downtown area was proposed for the Curb: the empty, city-owned lot on Main Street where the Opera House once stood. The lot was next to the City Hall, which was torn down just weeks before the Market opened in this location. J.C. Penney was later built on this historic spot, which now houses the Village Green Antique Mall.

While permission to locate on Main Street was finally granted by the City Council, some skepticism still remained about the Curb's likely success. In his Fiftieth Anniversary speech, FitzSimons declares, *"This was a new idea and there was much opposition at first. After a number of meetings, the city council reluctantly gave permission, but if I remember correctly, and I was at every meeting held, the city council in granting permission to use the city lot on Main Street expressed doubt as to the success of the project."*

The Hendersonville News offers more insight into what transpired. Preserved on microfilm at the Henderson County Public Library, a thorough study of these 1920s newspapers uncovers information on the Curb's historic Main Street beginning. The actual newspapers are archived with the Henderson County Genealogical & Historical Society located in downtown Hendersonville.

While newspapers from 1924 are silent about the Curb Market, numerous articles were written throughout the first half of 1925 which chronicle a number of important meetings and events concerning the Curb. These articles are printed in their entirety in the Appendix of this book, as are calendars for the purpose of clarity. The articles provide information which both confirms and adds to the Market's oral tradition. The following timeline of dates and titles establishes the pathway taken by the dedicated men and women who successfully founded the Curb Market.

It's understood that farm families came together in 1924 and started the

Curb. According to FitzSimons in his Fiftieth Anniversary speech, *"The Curb Market opened, as near as I can remember, the first or second week in June, 1924, fifty years ago."*

As the farm community worked together to grow and centralize the Market into a prime location, the first article on this subject appears in The Hendersonville News on Sunday, February 8, 1925, titled *"CURB MARKET COMING."* It states, *"The curb market is agitated again for Henderson county farmers. It had warm agitation two or three years ago but didn't have the agricultural 'pull' connected with it. I predict a 'go over' this time. County Agent Arnold and Home Agent, Miss Everett, will line up their forces and the thing will go over. Farmers and their wives will line up on the movement."*

Several days later, a second article appears on Wednesday, February 11, 1925, with a headline announcing, *"FARMERS WILL SELL AT CURB."* It begins, *"Henderson county farm products are to go direct from the grower to the customer without the customary peddling and knocking on the door from house to house. The curb market, the later and more approved method, is to be the solution to the problem."*

The next article is published on Sunday, March 8, 1925, and concerns an upcoming critical decision, *"CITY TO DECIDE ON CURB MARKET TUESDAY, MAR. 9."* While Tuesday would actually have been March 10, the body of information is clear. *"City commissioners are believed to look with favor upon the establishment of a curb market...*

"Mr. Arnold said the farmers would want to begin operating the curb May 1, and that the city owned vacant lot adjoining the city hall, he believed, suitable for the purpose until such time as the curb grew out of bounds. Two days a week, at first, will be designated as curb days."

The headline from Wednesday, March 11, 1925 reveals the milestone results of the meeting, *"CITY GIVES SITE TO FARMERS FOR CURB MARKET."* The article reads, *"Hendersonville's curb market will be opened for business about May 1, permission having been granted the county's farmers to use that part of the city's property next to the walls on the south side of the city hall. The building, however, will be torn down before that time.*

"County Agent Arnold went before the city commissioners and told them that the farmers wanted the opportunity to sell from a central place, and the commissioners willingly accepted."

A brief update occurs in the paper on Sunday, May 10, 1925, the only Curb Market headline without the usual all-capital letters, *"Curb Market Opens On Main Street On Saturday, May 16."* The article continues, *"Following announcement that the debris on the site of the old city hall property will be entirely cleared within the next few days, County Agent E. F. Arnold held a conference with the curb market committee of the farm bureau this afternoon, and regulations for the market are being completed, and a date set for the completion of the membership in that movement."*

As each obstacle was overcome, a date certain was finally determined, as revealed in this headline from Wednesday, May 20, 1925, *"SATURDAY, MAY 30, WILL MARK OPENING OF CURB MARKET IN THIS CITY; RULES ARE FIXED."* This article clarifies many issues. *"Hendersonville housewives will have the first opportunity at curb shopping and the farmers the first at curb marketing on Saturday, May 30. This decision was reached Saturday at a meeting of those interested in curb marketing.*

"Frank L. FitzSimons and E. F. Arnold reported in detail their findings on the Spartanburg curb market, which has been in successful operation for the past few years."

The last article before the Market opened for business on Main Street appears on Wednesday, May 27, 1925, titled *"PLANS COMPLETE FOR OPENING UP THE CURB MARKET."* It brings the community up to date. *"The board of control has been named, practically all arrangements completed, and plans made for parking of visitors and patrons for the curb market which will hold its initial sale Saturday, May 30, beginning at 7:30 a.m.*

"The market will open for its first sale at the hour stated, promptly, and crisp vegetables, dressed and live poultry, butter and eggs, cake, pie and flowers will be on sale. It is open to all farmers in the county who want to come in and sell their produce in this way.

"Chairman F. L. FitzSimons extends, as head of the board of control, an invitation to all housewives of the city to come out and pay the market a visit on the opening day."

The front page of the Sunday, May 31, 1925 newspaper carries an important headline, *"CURB MARKET OPENING FEATURED BY MANY HOME-GROWN PRODUCTS."* A description of the historic day follows. The article begins, *"'The opening of your curb market is a distinct credit to those who brought their produce and placed it on sale. I am well pleased to see the good beginning. It will naturally grow until you will have to provide permanent quarters.'*

"Mrs. Joseph Moody of Atlanta, a guest of the Cedars, thus gave expression to an interest in the subject after seeing notice of the opening in the press."

Several weeks later on Sunday, June 14, 1925, a photograph is front and center in The Hendersonville News. The caption above the picture reads, *"AS THE CURB MARKET APPEARS."* Underneath the photograph is a brief description. *"The above picture shows the Hendersonville curb market on its first opening two weeks ago. The two Saturdays since the opening have been featured by additional farm supplies and an increased number of customers. Housewives are finding it a desirable place for getting the freshest products at most attractive prices."*

This particular photograph shows two young women selling their produce on Main Street on opening day. Later on, the newspaper published a second photograph of this same scene, identical except there are three women instead of two. In both photographs, the young women are standing behind their vegetable stand, with a black Model T Ford parked nearby. The car is draped with handiwork for sale and is skirted with boxes of vegetables propped up against the running board and spoke wheels. The three women in the larger picture

First Curb Market Days
(Photo courtesy of the Curb Market)

are (L to R) Mildred Stepp, Daisy Henderson Pace, and Callie Case Walker. This photograph is a fascinating peek at the styles and realities of the mid-1920s and was captured on canvas in 1989 by talented and well-known local artist RuthEllen Boerman. Her iconic painting is titled "First Curb Market Days" and is on permanent display at the Curb, a tribute to and reminder of those who began this treasured enterprise.

As the history of the Curb Market has been chronicled and the anniversaries celebrated, 1924 is the acknowledged start year. Oral history: honored, revered and critical to the record has been handed down to each generation since FitzSimons and the first farm families joined together to start the Market. Today's vendors and descendents who trace their Curb Market lineage back to the earliest years are the keepers of this important legacy, a trust they hold dear. The Curb Market began in 1924 according to the mothers, fathers, grandparents, aunts and uncles who were there. They sold "from their farm wagons and from roadside stands on homemade tables under crude umbrellas," as the children of the original Curb families have described the Market's beginning. Their testimony stands. Uncovering the broader time-line as recorded in The Hendersonville News, however, allows a greater understanding and appreciation for their historic accomplishment. Clearly, May 30, 1925 could not have happened without the Market's existence in 1924.

Linda March wrote a wonderful article on the Curb Market for the April, 1994 issue of the Blue Ridge Business Journal, a Roanoke, Virginia newspaper. She includes an interview with Callie Walker in which Callie talks about FitzSimons and the establishment of the Market. March wrote, *"He helped the group receive the recognition and the attention it needed from the City to find a permanent location. This allowed the market to become an actual business concern which could profit in a unified way from the steady influx of visitors to the area."*

The Curb began because of the hard work, diligence, and creative efforts of the people, and the Curb is maintained that way today. This is the most important aspect of the Market's history. An early record claims that sales on the first day of business on Main Street totaled $23.31. In 1953, the Curb recorded $63,000 in annual sales. This total more than doubled and tripled in the peak years. The story at hand is the success of the Curb Market and the people who started and have kept that thread of industry and heritage weaving through the decades of life and economy in the mountains of Western North Carolina.

Chapter Three

Pioneer Families

Early Curb Market Scene
(Photo courtesy of the Curb Market)

Once the vote was taken by the city commissioners and permission was granted for the Curb Market to locate on Main Street, jubilation sparked the final push for opening day. In *From The Banks of The Oklawaha, Vol. II*, FitzSimons describes the preparations that brought Curb Market families together on May 30, 1925, the date established through the sequential events recorded and published that year in The Hendersonville News. Tables were quickly built for displaying the vegetables and the home-baked items that would be for sale. Supportive merchants donated large wagon umbrellas to protect produce and vendors from the sun. The Rigby - Morrow Company, a builder's supply and lumber business on Fourth Avenue East owned and operated by Foster Bennett and his son Roy, generously donated lumber, nails, and umbrellas to this endeavor. The County Farm Agent, Mr. E. F. Arnold, and the Home Demonstration Agent, Miss Rachel Everett, held meetings for farm families and members of the local 4-H Club for the purpose of instruction in the proper methods of preparing, grading and displaying the farm produce. The Curb would begin on a Saturday, with Tuesday and Thursday soon added to the schedule. Today, once Christmas and New Years are over, Saturday is again the only sale day until April arrives and the three-days-a-week schedule of 8:00 a.m. to 2:00 p.m. resumes.

FitzSimons recalls in his book, *"...only seven farmers and their wives brought produce to sell and the same seven were the only ones for several days* following...The Curb Market was successful from the beginning and more and more farmers applied for membership and the privilege of selling their farm products on the curb rather than peddling." (1)

Earl and Mary Marshall
(Photo courtesy of the Curb Market)

The list of all the vendors who sold on Main Street that first day of business has been lost. However, FitzSimons recalls the following families: Mr. and Mrs. W. W. Brown from Sugarloaf Road, Mr. and Mrs. Earl Marshall of Dana, a Mr. and Mrs. Jenkins, Mrs. Swift and her daughter from Upward, and Mr. and Mrs. Sam Pittillo from Fruitland. (2) They join the three young women in the photograph taken on that first Saturday: Mildred Stepp, Daisy Henderson Pace, and Callie Case Walker.

The Curb histories of these three women and their families are worth noting. The Pace family was at the Market for over 75 years through the involvement of Daisy and her husband Clarence, and their daughter Kathleen Pace Hammett. Clarence was on the Board of Control for 22 years.

Daisy's widowed mother was also a member of the Market for many years, Joanna Arledge Henderson, known as "Mother Henderson" by friends and family alike. She was a beloved figure in the Tracy Grove community where she lived. Her descendents are still active in the Curb today. Joanna's grandson Thomas (Daisy's nephew) and his wife Jane Duncan Henderson and their daughter Elizabeth are known far and wide for their farm-fresh produce. Their Curb Market tables are a popular, seasonal stop for both regular customers and visitors to the area.

Concerning the other two women in the famous photograph, Callie and her husband Grady, along with their daughter Patricia (Pat) Walker, represent 85 years of Curb history in 2009. For a number of years, Pat served as secretary on the Board of Control, and she still maintains a booth at the Market today. It's recorded that Mildred Stepp sold a chocolate layer cake for one dollar on opening day, promptly bought dress material with it, and spent the rest of her life as a faithful Curb Market customer.

In 1999, Pat Walker and her cousin, Terry Robinson, published *Members of the Henderson County Curb Market, 75 years of memories*. This booklet has been an invaluable historical resource and will be identified throughout the following chapters as the "book of memories." It is a compilation of brief memoirs and photos submitted by members of the Curb and their families in order to *"help preserve the memories of the friendships made and families represented over the last 75 years."*

One of the first entries concerns Mr. and Mrs. W. W. Brown (William W. and Maude Maxwell Brown), a memoir submitted by their eldest daughter, Laberta Brown Lamb. She describes her parent's Market offerings, representative of the variety found at the Curb. Laberta wrote, *"They had dressed chickens, rabbits, corn, beans, cabbage, potatoes, tomatoes, beets, radishes, and sometimes a hog...My grandmother, Mrs. Lula* (Hollingsworth) *Dill, made what she called drawn work, which consisted of pillowcases, scarves, tablecloths and napkins. We sold flowers such as asters, dahlia peonies, and all kinds of wild flowers and shrubs. The market is still being attended and has been a great help to the people of Henderson County."*

Dorothy and Albert King
(Photo courtesy of the Curb Market)

Another insightful story in the "book of memories" was penned by Dorothy Jackson King. She gives a meaningful glance into the effort her family made to participate in the earliest days of the Market. Dorothy was 15 years old in 1926 when she began selling at the Curb. She'd leave early in the morning with her family, setting out from their Dana home to arrive in time to claim a spot to sell their produce. *"I, along with Albert* (King), *my mother and father* (William and Lama Edney Jackson), *brothers and sisters arrived at the Curb Market from our home on Little Hungry Creek in a horse and wagon with our vegetables and chickens. Because selling space was allotted on a first come, first serve basis, we had to start our journey to town at about 4:00 a.m."* Dorothy and Albert married and *"raised seven children using the pay from the market as our main source of income."* This vendor line is still active at the Curb through Louise Jackson Hill and her cousins, Ralph and Charles King, and their respective families.

A brief history about another *"charter member of the Henderson County Curb Market,"* Dovie Louisa Justice Jones, is also found in the "book of memories." Dovie's granddaughter, Pearl A. King LeVar, wrote the memoir and later shared more information about her grandmother, who was born in 1885 to the Reverend John and Violet Taylor Justice. According to Pearl, on September 21, 1913 Dovie married 56 year old bachelor William Fanning Jones, who had delayed marrying until he had finished raising his brother's orphaned children. Over the next nine years, Dovie and William had five children of their own, and they were ages six years to 15 months old when William died. Pearl wrote, *"Dovie became a widow on July 10, 1922 and struggled to raise her five children."* (Is the word "struggle" an understatement to anyone else?!) Fortunately, the Curb Market would provide a way for Dovie to support her family. For 50 years, *"She sold fruits and vegetables from her garden, jams and jellies, aprons, and potholders."*

I wanted to learn more about this courageous woman, and Pearl was pleased to share some of the details of her grandmother's marriage and life. "Dovie lived a hard life," Pearl said clearly over the phone one day. "She grew her own vegetables and would plow her garden with a horse, just like a man, growing whatever she thought she could sell. She sold gooseberries and blackberries, and the first money I ever made came from picking blackberries and selling them at the Curb Market. Dovie had her own chickens, too, and if we had five cents for every feather we've plucked, we'd be rich! We plucked chicken feathers every Monday, Wednesday and Friday nights. She'd then soak the chickens in salt water overnight to take to Market the next day. In the evenings, Dovie would sew clothes for her children."

Pearl continued her story, "My mother, Violet Jones King, was her daughter. I grew up helping my grandmother at the Curb, where Uncle Andrew would take us in the mornings. After the close, we'd carry our empty baskets to the city bus station, where we'd catch a bus to Dana to be dropped off at the Stepp Store. My uncle would pick us up there and take us home. Dovie was in her late-80s when she finally stopped selling. She died when she was 89."

The history of the Curb Market is the history of the people: their lives, their circumstances, their hard work and accomplishments. Since facets of Dovie's life are common to that era, her story provides fascinating insight into a period of time which is, frankly, incomprehensible in this modern age. We're basically left to wonder about the ones who started the Curb Market, the strength, diligence and sacrifice of these pioneers, as they've been called.

They were fortunate to be able to participate in this economic opportunity: the hard-working farmer and his wife, the single individual, and the widow with a family to raise and support.

From the beginning, a manager has kept the Curb Market running efficiently, interacting with both the individual members as well as with the Board of Control. In the "book of memories," there is information about several of the managers, beginning with Coela Lyda Coston, the third person to hold this position. Mrs. K. Jenkins was the first manager, and Mrs. C.N. Cady briefly succeeded her. Coela began selling at the Market when it was still on Main Street. She was known for her butter, eggs and preserves, her table enhanced in the summer months with selected vegetables from her garden. Coela was hired as the manager in 1926 and kept this position until her death in 1966, at age 65. In the "book of memories," Coela's daughters, Leola Coston Marlowe and Kathleen Coston Hodges, describe their mother's responsibilities as manager as well as the chores their father, Robert L. Coston, attended to in the early years.

"The manager's duties were posting prices as they often changed, collecting 5 percent of sales on each market day, keeping individual records, selling paper bags, and making change. Also included was building fires in the tall pot bellied stoves and sweeping the aisles after market hours. Our father, with a little help from us, looked after these chores."

Leola also writes her own personal memoir in the "book of memories," revealing the successful contribution the women of the Curb Market made to the economic stability of their families. Working either alone, with their parents, or side-by-side with their husbands, the early years of the Market provided a natural outlet for the talents and industry of this generation or two of women who might have hesitated to take a job in the community. Leola reveals the delightful fashion sense of the women proud to be seen and working at the Curb.

"At age eighty, there's much to be recalled. As the market grew and became organized the farm wives had a chance to use their abilities to help provide a better living, install indoor plumbing, buy modern appliances, and help provide better education for the children. It wasn't an easy way! It meant long hard hours – lots of determination! We have been truly blessed in this endeavor.

"It's fun to reminisce on how we dressed. Nearly all wore hats, pill boxes, broad brims, flowers, feathers, and bows. Yes, there have been many changes! We hope we have been helpful to our city friends and visiting tourists."

Unquestionably, vendors faithful to their tasks, creative in their crafts, and consistent in the unsurpassed quality of their products have had a far-reaching and enduring impact here, usually beyond their knowing. Sometimes, there's a glimpse into what the Curb means to its customers. On an unusually cool yet delightfully pleasant July 1 morning, 2008, Libby Wright from Charleston, South Carolina, stopped at the Curb Market to purchase one of Marilyn Horne's Caramel Cakes. Her views on Marilyn's cakes and her memories of the Market confirm the uniqueness of this special place.

"Marilyn Horne's Caramel Cake has a reputation that goes throughout the Southeast," Libby pronounced decidedly. "When my sixteen year old grandson arrived yesterday, the first thing he asked for when he got out of the car was for one of her cakes!

"I've been coming to the Curb Market all my life, and I'm now 77 years old," she declared. "Since I was a little girl, we've been coming up from Charleston each summer to our home in Flat Rock. It was a big thing to come to the Market. My mother bought everything here: cottage cheese, chicken, eggs, ham, sausage, vegetables, milk, and butter. There were even boxes of puppies and kittens, free. I remember saving glass jars to give to Joyce Pace for her preserves. Yes, it's a big thing to come here."

Indeed it is.

As this book was nearing publication, notice was received concerning the deaths of Paul and Kathleen Pace Hammett, daughter of Clarence and Daisy Henderson Pace. Kathleen died on July 13, 2010, the day after her husband of 71 years, Paul G. Hammett, died on July 12, 2010.

Chapter Four

From Under the Umbrellas

The Curb Market (Building) on King Street
(Photo courtesy of the Curb Market)

Organization has always been paramount to the success of the Curb Market. A Board of Control was established early on to determine the rules and regulations necessary to run the Market. Frank L. FitzSimons was elected the first Chairman of the Board and held that position for 15 years. Along with FitzSimons, the original Board members were Mrs. A.F. Coleman from Tracey Grove, Mrs. Earl (Mary Justice) Marshall of Dana, Mr. D.P. Moss from Edneyville, Mrs. John Redden of Crab Creek, and Mrs. S.P. Williamson from Mills River.

The combined efforts of FitzSimons, Hollowell, the county agents, the farm families who participated and the customers who supported them led to a resounding success. So much for predictions of failure! The Curb Market quickly outgrew its Main Street location, prompting the Board to purchase a lot on King Street in 1926. The lot was lower than street level and tucked behind the American Drug Company, now closed, and the synagogue, which belonged to the Agudas Israel Congregation. (The Jewish congregation was founded in 1922 and purchased a building on King Street in 1925 to renovate for their synagogue. In 2002, Agudas Israel moved into their new synagogue on Glasgow Lane in Laurel Park. The Salvation Army Family Store and Donation Center is now in their old location.)

When the Curb Market moved to King Street, a new and expanded phase of commerce began with the construction of a building to house the Market. Laberta Lamb explains in her "book of memories" account, *"The people donated lumber and other building materials, and the people did the work. Now the market could be held year round."* The Rigby - Morrow Company also generously donated material for the initial Curb Market building. According to a brief history written in 1940 by Coela Coston, Curb Manager, *"They* (the Rigby-Morrow Company) *were the first to help us from under an umbrella to a neat building. Later, as the demand for more space became greater, the building was enlarged."*

Inside the early Curb Market
(Photo courtesy of the Curb Market)

Vendors were responsible for keeping their table and area clean and for observing the stated rules, one of which undoubtedly saved the Market a lot of grief over the years: *"Any person found gossiping, tattling, causing confusion or disturbances in the market while the market is open for business may be called before the board of control and punished as the board of control may decide."*

A vendor paid a 5% sales-day commission to sell at the Curb Market. This practice was eventually replaced with a yearly fee for stock holders, who own one stock each at the cost of $1.00. According to French "Pop" Rogers, who was involved with the Market for over 50 years and held the position of treasurer for over half that time, a bank wouldn't lend money for repairs or updates based on commission income alone. A fixed, once-a-year fee for members solved that problem.

Today, along with the yearly fee, a stock holder is allowed to rent up to two tables, although additional tables belonging to other family members may be used. Over the years, with Board approval, these booths have passed to children and relatives upon the retirement or death of a Curb Market member. There are descendents of the early farm families currently active at the Curb, but many of the tables belong to individuals or families without this connection. Eligibility is determined by the Board and is based on residence in Henderson County, where products are home-grown and home-made. New members are welcomed and appreciated, as are the day-renters who also have an opportunity to sell here.

The Market was an Association until 1933 and operated by *"mutual agreement,"* wrote Coela Coston in her brief history. With 101 tables and 120 sellers at that point, success required legal incorporation under the laws of North Carolina. (1) Thus the Curb Market became a non-profit farmers' cooperative organization with a five-member board. It also became a model for other communities interested in starting a similar operation. The original incorporators were Sam J. Pittillo, Mrs. L. V. Lyda, Mrs. Lila C. (Dalton) Hill, J. A. Lytle and Clarence Pace. The corporate record is dated January 21, 1933 and was signed and sealed in the presence of Noah Hollowell. The capital stock was 990 shares of $1 par value.

Coela Coston, Curb Market Manager
(Photo courtesy of the Curb Market)

Bylaws were written giving the Board of Control *"full and complete charge of the Curb Market at all times."* Ersie Griffin Ratliff Davis was manager of the Curb in 1974 when she, too, recorded some of the Market's history. She describes the importance of the by-laws, *"The market owes much of its success to the determination and foresight of the pioneers who worked so diligently during the depression years to formulate by-laws which were necessary to determine and insure the rights of each individual."*

By the late 1930s, the Curb Market had outgrown its King Street location. A brief article appears in The Times-News on Saturday, December 31, 1938, touching on the Market's permanent move to the corner of Church Street and Second Avenue. *"CURB MARKET HAS BIG YEAR,"* and *"Officers Re-elected and Plans Are Laid for New Building"* is the informative header. The entire article is in the Appendix, but it begins, *"The Farmers Mutual Curb Market members re-elected officers today, made arrangements to raze the building and erect a new one on Church Street, and heard a report from the manager that showed a banner year of $28,024.98."*

According to the June 28, 1978 article in The Times-News on the history and growth of the Curb Market, *"ground was broken for a new building on January 1, 1939. The razing of the King Street building was started the next day and in the interim, the Market rented the Brooks Building (southeast corner of Third and Church) for use as the market and also rented the lot north of the new building for a year to serve as a parking area both for vendors and customers. A frame building was erected to house the market by the summer season of 1939."*

The Curb Market settled into its new building, an attractive white clapboard structure with numerous twelve-pane, double-hung windows positioned low enough so vendors could pass their goods straight from their vehicles to their booths. The Curb was now permanently situated behind and across the street from the Henderson County Courthouse and Jail. This chosen location on the corner of Church Street and Second Avenue already had an unusual history: it was once the site for the public hangings which took place during the last half of the 1800s. With the jailhouse windows overlooking this corner, the sights and sounds accompanying the construction of the gallows were not lost on the men who could watch or listen as the frame took shape. Gallows were built for those convicted of serious, first degree crimes, and in Vol. 1 of his trilogy, *From The Banks of The Oklawaha*, FitzSimons has recorded the stories of several famous hangings. When the Curb Market took up residence on this location, nearly 50 years had passed since the final hanging. During that time, the property was used primarily as a wood yard.

The Curb Market's new home was replaced in 1955 with a more substantial, brick building. A news-worthy announcement on April 21, 1955 accompanies a picture of the original wooden structure and declares, *"THIS BUILDING, home of the Mutual Curb Market for several years, has been razed and foundations are being poured for the proposed new building on the site of the old, but of brick and concrete blocks, much larger and more commodious in order to accommodate more growers who might better supply the growing list of customers. Meanwhile business is carried on in the Farmers Market Building in Southside, Greenville Road and White Street."*

Just prior to this announcement, Mrs. Raymond Pace wrote an article for The Times-News that appeared on Friday, April 15, 1955 titled *"ARDUOUS ENDEAVOR TELLS DEVELOPMENT STORY OF HENDERSON COUNTY CURB MARKET."* In her account, Mrs. Pace revisits the history of the Curb, giving recognition to the two original county agents at the inception of the Market, Mr. E. F. Arnold and Miss Rachel Everett. She also adds, *"We have always received wholehearted support from other farm agents through the years such as O. B. Jones, G. D. White and our present farm agent, D. W. Bennett."*

Mrs. Pace ends her article with a heartfelt portrayal of the Curb Market, one worth sharing. *"We are justly proud of the market which represents many years of struggle and hardship. Some still attend the market who were active in its very early years, others are not there any more (sic), but their efforts are appreciated because it was during those early years that the way was paved for us to enter into the opportunities that we are now offered. The present members, too, wish to make sacrifices if necessary that we may contribute to the future generations for a bigger and better Henderson County and City of Hendersonville.*

"In view of these facts a contract has been let for a modern building with the necessary equipment for the operation of the market (at) its present location on Church Street.

"The market not only offers a means for the farmers and their families to make a livelihood and educate their children and accommodate the city folks and tourist but it brings city and county, also people from different states together in a mutual friendship and understanding. Many friendships are found that would not have existed had they not met at the Curb Market."

Three months later on Wednesday, July 20, 1955, a photograph and description of the completed building was published in the newspaper. The announcement reads, *"THE NEW MODERN HENDERSON COUNTY MUTUAL CURB MARKET—The building costing around $40,000 is of yellow brick construction, measuring 47 x 157 feet. Many windows give excellent lighting and ventilation to the spacious building. Located on North Church Street. Ample parking space solves the customer's parking problems."*

This new building went without any major exterior change until the spring of 2008, when it was topped with a peaked roof of attractive green metal, complete with cupola and traditional cockerel weathervane.

Driving south on Church Street, you can't miss the Curb on the right. It's the place where history comes alive every week of the year. Be sure and stop!

The Curb Market (Building) on Church Street - 1940
(Photo courtesy of the Curb Market)

Chapter Five
Memories from Golden Glow Farm
Frank L. FitzSimons Jr. and his son, Frank L. FitzSimons III
Homage to the Founder

Frank Lockwood FitzSimons
(Photo courtesy of Frank L. FitzSimons III)

Golden Glow Farm has been lovingly described as a home place *"surrounded by relatives, rose gardens and apple orchards."* (1) That's still true today. The Dana farm was the residence for Frank L. FitzSimons Sr. and his wife of 56 years, Margarita "Maggie" Kershaw, great-great-granddaughter of Judge Mitchell King, who donated land for the city of Hendersonville. While Frank Sr. has been gone since 1980, his son, Frank L. FitzSimons Jr., 83 in 2008, still lives on family property just down the road from his father's picturesque home. Frank L. FitzSimons III, known as either Hank or Frank, and his wife Carmen are preparing to move into his grandfather's house. Golden Glow Farm continues to be the residence for other family members as well.

"We understand Pa's yellow house was built in 1848," Hank said about his grandfather's home. "It still has the wide floor boards and the bead board that was so popular. Only the kitchen has been remodeled."

It was a bright summer morning when we sat with his father, Frank Jr., in his own lovely home, bordered by abundant apple orchards framed by the distant and commanding Blue Ridge Mountains. The view immediately brought to mind Psalm 121:1-2, *"I will lift up mine eyes unto the hills, from whence cometh my help. My help cometh from the Lord, which made heaven and earth."* I could well imagine I wasn't the first to think of those comforting verses as I gazed out the big picture window at the unending blue ridge of mountains that rimmed the unending green line of apple trees. It was breathtaking.

Hank continued, "Pa (as he called his grandfather) started his dairy farm after he returned from service in France, where he was stationed during World War I. He was in the Navy; so was my daddy, and so was I." (2)

Frank Jr. explained, "After the start of World War II, I joined the Navy as soon as I could and was in the Pacific on a PT boat. I had a hand in naming the boat 'The Carolina Queen,' because the boat was financed by war bonds sold in North Carolina. I even have a picture."

And sure enough, Hank produced a marvelous black and white photograph of "The Carolina Queen" racing the waves, with Frank Jr. standing on top, the wind strong, and the experience exhilarating. I could only marvel at the rarity of owning such a priceless picture.

Frank Jr. shared another unusual wartime story, this one concerning his best friend. "I grew up with Bill McKay, and we were both in the Pacific at the same time, except he was in submarines," he explained. "We even dated the same girl working at a USO canteen in Brisbane, Australia, where we would go for R&R. It was a surprise to learn she became engaged to a boy from Henderson County, who just happened to be my best friend Bill McKay!" As it turned out, there was no engagement, but the coincidence makes a wonderful story which FitzSimons enjoys sharing.

The relationship between the families began when William "Bill" McKay was very young, and his parents (Lawrence H. and Mary Smyth McKay) started farming in Tracy Grove, not far from the FitzSimons' homestead. Bill and Frank Jr., both born in 1925, grew up sharing the personal milestones and events of their generation.

When Bill died in late March, 2008, Jessica Goodman interviewed Frank Jr. and his son for a Times-News article. She wrote, *"FitzSimons and McKay continued on a similar path after the war, both graduating from Clemson, working on their family farm, getting bank jobs, joining the Kiwanis Club. 'Bill and I were just best friends all of our lives,' (Frank Jr.) said...'You couldn't ask for a finer person,' (Frank III) fondly recalled."*

Along with an abiding friendship between the sons, a significant, historical bond exists between the FitzSimons and the McKay families. They are connected to some of the most important places and organizations in Henderson County. McKay served the people of Henderson County in a number of meaningful ways. He was on the school board for 21 years and was a founding trustee for the Blue Ridge Community College, originally known as Henderson County Technical Institute. McKay's great-grandfather, Captain Ellison Adger Smyth (1847-1942), was a pioneer in the southern textile industry and brought his expertise from South Carolina to Henderson County. Smyth was a Confederate Army veteran who, along with his son James Adger Smyth, Mary's father, founded Balfour Mills in 1924 (now Kimberly-Clark Corporation – Berkeley Mills). This would turn out to be a momentous year for the community, as the Curb Market also began in 1924 under the inspiration and guidance of Frank FitzSimons Sr. and Noah Hollowell.

Frank and Maggie FitzSimons walking at Golden Glow Farm
(Photo courtesy of Frank L. FitzSimons III)

Captain Smyth was familiar with this area, having purchased Connemara in 1900, the farm in Flat Rock once known as Rock Hill and previously owned by Christopher G. Memminger, Confederate treasurer. Connemara was sold to Carl Sandburg in 1945, several years after Smyth's death. Today, the Carl Sandburg Home National Historic Site is run by The National Park Service and is treasured for its hiking trails, for the Sandburg legacy that includes their legendary goat herd, and for its mountainous beauty. The FitzSimons and McKay families intertwine with Henderson County's 20th century history like few other families do. Their impact for good on this community is incalculable.

After reminiscing about his best friend, Frank Jr. was happy to discuss life as he knew it growing up on Golden Glow Farm with his younger sister, Margarita FitzSimons Allston. "Daddy grew produce and ran a dairy, but he also taught school." He added incredulously, "I don't see how he did it! When I got to be 16, I started a truck farm business with my own route. I had a Model-T Ford and learned to drive it so I could deliver my produce to stores, boarding houses and hotels. In those days, there weren't the vegetables in the stores that you see today, so people would usually buy directly from the farms. The Curb was an option for farmers, but I didn't have a table. Tom and Milda Orr, our neighbors and good friends, were vendors who would sell the produce grown by Tom and Daddy together. Mama and Milda would prepare the vegetables and help bring them to market.

"When the war was over," Frank Jr. continued, "I went to Marshall College for a year then transferred to Clemson, where I graduated in 1949 with a degree in Agricultural Engineering. Bill and I were there together. After college, I married Clara Mather FitzSimons from Savannah, Georgia. She was my third cousin and already a FitzSimons. I went on to a career in banking which I combined with farming, something I've done all my life."

Frank III was born in 1950, and another son followed, Samuel Dunkin FitzSimons. Their mother, Clara, died when Hank was in the 10th grade. Frank Jr. eventually married Millie Jones Priest, and she and her three daughters became part of the family at Golden Glow Farm. "It was a privilege growing up here, where Daddy raised cattle, crops, and children," Hank said with a smile. "After high school, I joined the Navy, and after that I went to Clemson. I graduated from there in 1976 and married Carmen Ochoa, who was a student from Guatemala, Central America. We have two daughters and one grandson. I finished my Master's degree in 1984 in Agricultural Education and worked for the Clemson Extension Service for 26 years before retiring in 2003. I have a home in Summerville, South Carolina."

Reflecting on his family's role in founding the Curb Market, Hank thoughtfully stated, "I remember my grandfather; he was always in the background. He was Big Frank, my daddy was Frankie, and the family called me Hank. My grandfather was a humble man who never talked much or bragged about his accomplishments, but he considered the creation of the farmers' market his greatest accomplishment. He brought the centralized, open-air market concept back to Henderson County from his wartime experience in France, and now the Curb is an historic, key site for tourists and residents alike. Thank goodness it's still strong after all these years."

At the Curb Market's 65th Anniversary festivities, Hank's grandmother Maggie remarked, *"I think it's grand the way people pitched in and helped with the celebration. A lot of them wouldn't have done without (the Curb Market)."*

Dwight Bennett, retired Henderson County Agricultural Extension Chairman, also made an observation on the 65th Anniversary, *"The Curb Market has done as much for the people in the county as anything else. It's one of the greatest institutions in the county."*

Frank L. FitzSimons Sr., his family, and each person who has contributed to the success of the Market deserve all the gratitude a community can give for their enterprising vision and effort. To each one, "Thank you."

Sadly, Frank L. FitzSimons Jr. died on November 16, 2009 at age 84. In a Times-News article by Jessica Goodman, FitzSimons is remembered *"as a Southern gentleman who, like his father, had a knack for storytelling, loved farming and became active in many aspects of civic life...'He was a stalwart of the community,' said Frank FitzSimons III, one of Frank's two sons. 'He was just a great family man who loved his extended family and gathering together at the holidays.'"*

The obituary for Frank Jr. recognizes his remarkable career of service, demonstrating the power of his father's example. Frank Jr. was on the board of directors for the Flat Rock Playhouse, the Chamber of Commerce, the Henderson County Library Board and the Apple Festival Committee. Frank Jr. was also a lifetime member and past president of the Kiwanis Club. There is a familiar and fitting proverb that applies well to this family, "The apple doesn't fall far from the tree." Indeed.

Chapter Six

Managing the Market
French and Bobbi Hill Rogers
Raised Under the Table

French and Bobbi Rogers (Photo courtesy of the Curb Market)

As of 2009, there have been nine individuals hired to manage the Curb Market. Several have served as manager for a short time; others for a very long time. During the first year and a half, Mrs. K. Jenkins and Mrs. C. N. Cady held this position. Mrs. Coela Coston managed the Market from 1926 to 1966, followed by Mrs. Barbrea "Bobbi" Hill Rogers. Mrs. Ersie Griffin Ratliff Davis was the manager from 1968 to 1990. Lois Kerr Taylor served next, then Lois Bishop Sawick. Dan Volkert took the position in 1994 and was manager until his untimely death in 2001, when his assistant Elaine Duncan Staton accepted the responsibility.

Bobbi Rogers became the manager after Coela's death, a position she maintained for several years. Once a child at her parent's Curb Market booth, Bobbi was *"raised under the table,"* as she describes it in the "book of memories." She explains, *"One of my earliest memories is from sitting under the table with a small basket of June apples and asking customers if they would like to buy some!"*

Her grandparents were John K. and Rosa Revis Hill, lovingly called "Mama Hill," and they lived in Dana near the grade school. Rosa modeled the life of a busy farm wife bringing a litany of recorded offerings to the Curb, *"eggs, butter, buttermilk, cottage cheese, jellies, jams, grapes, raspberries, blackberries, huckle berries (sic), cut flowers, plants, extra garden vegetables, rhubarb, apples, walnuts, and ham."* Bobbi added a noteworthy piece of rural history in her memoir, *"Milk, butter and eggs were kept cool in the basements till electricity came to Dana in the spring of 1936."* Bobbi and her husband, French "Pop" Rogers, received Rosa's table when she retired in 1952.

Bobbi's parents, Raymond and Eura Coston Hill, began selling at the Curb Market around 1926 and sold until Raymond's death ten years later. Eura continued selling, and when she remarried in 1945 her second husband, Herbert L. Davis, became an active member, even serving as Chairman of the Board of Control in the late 1960s. Eura and Herbert had a son, John, who also grew up at the Curb. In his "book of memories" entry, John wrote, *"I helped prepare goods to sell and man the table with my parents."* John's wife Evelyn became active, eventually acquiring her own booth where she added quilts to her garden offerings. Eura died in 1978 after more than 50 years at the Curb.

There was a story to be told about this family, so I headed to Dana one summer morning in 2008. Pop and I sat on the front porch of their Dana home, the fields and apple orchards spreading before us under the hot August sun. He began with unfortunate news, "Last January, Bobbi fell and broke her left leg below the knee," Pop explained sadly. "She's still in a nursing home, unable to walk. It's been a difficult time. She was 82 in July, born in the house next door. Her grandfather and daddy established this apple orchard around 100 years ago. Her parents would peddle their apples and produce in town before they joined the Curb Market, which they did within a year after it started on Main Street. Bobbi was with them, *'under the table,'* as she says."

Pop continued, "I was born April 8, 1924 in Fontana, in Swain County. I went into the Navy during World War II and was on an aircraft carrier as a medic. After being discharged in 1946, I went back to Berea College in Kentucky and met this beautiful red-haired girl, Bobbi. I've always been partial to red hair," Pop chuckled. "We graduated and got married in 1949 at the First (United) Methodist Church in Hendersonville and then left for the University of Illinois in Champaign. We both got our Master's degrees, and I went on to teach math and science at Edneyville High School for 30 years. Bobbi worked in pre-school and kindergarten at Dana Elementary for 25 years, all the while maintaining a table at the Curb. When we left Illinois we had our degrees, a car and nothing else. The little house Bobbi was born in was empty because her mother had remarried, so we were able to live there. We eventually bought and remodeled this house."

Ray Rogers
(Photo by Ann Wirtz)

He added, "Our son, Ray, was born in 1953. He has our booth at the Curb Market now, where he sells gemstones which he cuts and polishes himself. He sets them into bolos, pins, necklaces, that kind of thing. The stones come from this area and from all over the world. We also had a second son, John, who died in 1992."

On a busy "Ol' Timey Days" celebration the last Saturday in September, Ray took time to share his Curb Market story. His display cases were alive with the intricate design, color and beauty only polished gemstones can give. When walking past his booth, the eye sweeps over the array of jewelry and pieces Ray has meticulously created, and awe is the normal response. It's my response to his work. So much so, I eventually bought a beautiful, white moonstone pendant, a delight to wear.

That busy morning, however, dried flower bouquets were also available at his table, freshly bundled for the autumn season: straw flowers, pepper grass and assorted kind grown, gathered and presented for sale. I bought a bouquet that perfectly enhanced the pottery vase given to me by my son and daughter-in-law, Arie Todd and Dewa. As I studied the offerings at his booth,

Ray explained how he helped his grandmother with the plants she raised and sold, and how he has kept the gardens going. "I do cut flowers, too," he added, "hydrangeas, lilacs and peonies. All of this is part of my life. I enjoy being here, doing what I can to support the Market, covering tables when others aren't here, just helping however I can."

After 30 years, Ray is now retired from managing the local movie theaters. He lives with his dad and visits and cares for his mother. The essence of this man can be summed up in one word: faithful. Ray has been a faithful son and grandson, employee, and member of the Curb Market.

The day I met with Pop, he shared some closing thoughts about his family and the Curb, so integral to their lives. "I'm proud of my son Ray, grateful for all he's done, ecstatic that he's taken over our booth. You see, he's carrying on for us. When I retired from teaching in 1980, I attended the annual meeting here and was both nominated to be on the Board and then elected to be the treasurer. I didn't want my name to just be on the roll, I have to be active if I'm a member. I loved serving in this position and held it until 2006. Mostly though, I've been Bobbi's chauffeur, bringing her to the Curb. She learned well from her mother and grandmother. We've loved this place."

On Saturday, August 2, 2008, a retirement party was given to acknowledge and honor French Rogers, Hoyte Jones and Joyce Pace for their more than 50 years of participation in the Curb Market. These three will be greatly missed, four counting Bobbi, each one part of the colorful fabric that is the history of the Curb.

Another end of an era occurred when Barbrea Hill Rogers died on July 17, 2010. Our condolences go to French, Ray, and the family.

Chapter Seven

The Storybook Dolls Lady
Ersie Griffin Ratliff Davis
Manager for 22 Years

Ersie Ratliff Davis, Ol' Timey Days
(Photo courtesy of the Curb Market)

It was now the end of November, and I was attending the annual "Ol' Timey Christmas" festivities. The Market was filled with people enjoying hot apple cider and cookies. With cup in hand, they'd pause at the various booths to admire and purchase the eye-catching decorations, the holly and greenery, the various foods and desserts, and the clever creativity that promised answers to decorating and gift dilemmas. The holiday atmosphere was enhanced by the carols which floated from the sound system and mingled with the conversation and laughter enlivening each aisle.

Punctuating the air was the distinct jingle of sleigh bells worn by Dan, the beautiful, black Percheron horse owned by James (Red) and Judy Seay from Misty View Carriage Rides of Hendersonville. Red was driving and Dan was pulling a handsome carriage loaded with passengers eager for a ride under a cloudy, it-could-snow-any-minute sky. Getting in the mood for the holidays is easy to do at "Ol' Timey Christmas" Day at the Curb Market!

Misty View Carriage Rides, James (Red) and Judy Seay
(Photo by Ann Wirtz)

Before lining up for my own carriage ride, I went inside the Market for some hot cider to keep me warm and to purchase a box of note cards from my dear friend, RuthEllen Boerman. I specifically wanted the note cards representing her series of paintings on the 23rd Psalm. As we were talking, a lady stopped by the adjoining booth belonging to Phyllis Rhodes from Rhodes Farm and Crafts. Phyllis makes a variety of soft toys and dolls. Her Little Red Riding Hood three-in-one doll was on display and caught this woman's attention. "Oh," she said reverently, "this doll reminds me of my childhood. I used to have a doll like this, one I purchased here. This brings back wonderful memories."

Ersie Griffin Ratliff Davis, a.k.a. the Storybook Dolls Lady, would be pleased. She was very likely the one who made the doll of this sweet memory. While several women created storybook dolls back then, Ersie made and sold untold number of them throughout her nearly 64 years of involvement at the Curb Market. Ersie was manager of the Curb for 22 of those years, from 1968 until 1990, but her work didn't keep her from designing and sewing some of the most unusual dolls ever made. Her storybook dolls are known as Topsy-Turvy, Flip-It, Upside Down or Three-in-One dolls, unique because they are actually several characters in one, revealed when the doll is turned over. Ersie made a variety of famous personalities, including Dorothy with the Lion, Scarecrow and Tin Man, and Goldilocks with the Three Bears.

In a 1988 article for the Times-News titled, *"Bakkers doll comes with a surprise ending,"* author Roann Bishop features Davis and the Curb Market as a must see during Henderson County's 42nd Annual North Carolina Apple Festival, held on Labor Day weekend. In the article, Ersie Ratliff Davis, 74, shares some of her Curb Market memories, *"'I started coming right after high school in them Depression years. I didn't get to go to college or anything. I liked to sew, and I started making little black and white dolls. From that I expanded to all the storybook dolls. I just think them up and make them.*

"'I made eight dolls Monday, and that was a hard day's work. But I can't keep them,' she said. 'I've got orders now that I've got to fill.'"

Her first doll was created in 1937 on the old treadle sewing machine that she was still using in 1988. *"'I never did care for an electric sewing machine,'"* she told Bishop.

Perhaps the most unusual doll she ever made was the Jim and Tammy Faye Bakker doll mentioned in the title. *"'Everybody comes by to see it,' Davis said of the cotton batting-stuffed doll that features Jim on one end, flips over to show Tammy with fur cape and bright red embroidered lips and fingernails on the opposite end, and a bespectacled Jessica Hahn on the back side of Tammy.*

"'People down here come by and look at it and bring people to see it,' she said. 'I really don't care to sell it because it's a lot of extra work. With all her jewelry and furs and fixing his suit, it takes almost a full day to make one of these.'"

Bishop writes, *"The Jim, Tammy and Jessica doll is just the latest in Davis' collection of homemade dolls, most of which are patterned after storybook characters, such as Little Red Riding Hood, which flips over to expose grandma. Pull grandma's nightcap down and there's the big, bad wolf."*

Ersie adds, *"'Red Riding Hood is the most popular doll. I had nine of them this morning, and I've got one left.'"*

"For Davis, making the dolls provides pleasure as well as profit," Bishop observes.

"'I'm a widow; I live alone,' she said. 'These dolls are a pastime as well as a way of making a living.'"

Ersie's "book of memories" entry expands on her Curb experience and describes life in Henderson County in the 1930s, a familiar narrative for many. *"I graduated from Fruitland Institute in 1931 during the depression. There was no work, nor money. I worked two years in Hendersonville in boarding houses for $2.50 a week, which was seven days a week. My dad said he would buy a car if I would learn to drive. Neither he nor my mother could drive. He bought a used car – a 1931 roadster for $100.00. I learned to drive. We started to the Curb Market in 1936, just on weekdays, for there were no tables empty on Saturday. I started out with farm produce; then my mother made bonnets. Later, I started making dolls – a first. I designed the storybook dolls, which are still popular on the market. After I married in 1945, and my son was born in 1948, we started slingshots and gee haa whemney diddles (sic) for him to sell – and also Indian corn – another first...I started at the market at 21 years old and still have crafts there at 85 years old."*

The ol' timers remember and admire Ersie for her dolls and her excellence as a manager. She has said about the people of the Curb Market, *"You get used to everybody. It's just like being with home folks."* Others would wholeheartedly agree.

Chapter Eight
Maintaining the Flow
Stanley and Elaine Duncan Staton
Woodworking, Pound Cakes and the Current Manager

Elaine Staton, Current Curb Market Manager
(Photo by Ann Wirtz)

"We've only been here since 1998, so we're relative newcomers," Elaine Duncan Staton explained as she sat behind the manager's desk, centrally located in the midst of the Curb Market activity. It was a Tuesday morning and traffic was light enough she could take time to share her story. As the current manager of the Curb, Elaine chatted with me as she also attended to the duties that maintain the flow of operation. She was occasionally interrupted to make change, answer the telephone, speak on the intercom, answer questions, sell items for an absent vendor, or even to sell one of her own pound cakes, too tempting for me to pass up. Early in our conversation I had wisely picked out half of a lemon cake and set it aside, because by the end of our time together, only one pound cake was left, and it didn't last long.

Yes, I couldn't resist, and the cake turned out to be as delicious as it looked. I shared some with my dear friend Sylvia Frank, who was well-known several years ago as an informal spokeswoman for Hendersonville's Pine Park Retirement Inn. She accurately calls pound cake, "The Ultimate Cake." Sylvia raved about Elaine's dessert, "I loved it! I cut it in small pieces to make it last longer." (Now, if I appear to digress some throughout this book, it's only to demonstrate the joyful and meaningful impact Curb Market product has on our lives!)

Elaine's warm and friendly way with customers and vendors alike was quite evident the morning we spoke together. Fortunately, there were enough quiet moments for her to explain how she and Stanley became part of the Curb Market family. Myrtle Lyda Rogers was a friend from their home church, Fruitland United Methodist, and she encouraged them to become vendors. Myrtle had inherited a table in the early 1980s from her Aunt Minnie Owenby Whiteside. Minnie had been selling at the Market since it was located on King Street, where she offered a variety of food as well as chicken-shaped potholders, sunbonnets and aprons. An active member of St. Paul's Episcopal Church near her home in Edneyville, Aunt Minnie was still making items for her table when she died at age 93.

Myrtle continued a similar tradition with her own creative sewing, much of which was original, artistic designs of bonnets, aprons, and American Girl doll clothes. She considered Elaine and Stanley a perfect fit for the Market after seeing the beauty and quality of Stanley's woodworking, which covers everything from shelves and stools to baby cradles and bowls, including delicate scroll saw work.

Elaine explained, "Most of what Stanley made back then we simply gave away as gifts. We finally decided to try selling his pieces, and since there were some tables available here, Myrtle really pushed for us to come. She even wrote a letter to the Board on our behalf. We wrote a letter, too, and brought some of Stanley's product for them to evaluate. Several weeks later we got a call from Pat Walker, the Board Secretary, informing us we were accepted as vendors.

"She then asked if I ever made pound cakes which, of course, I had but I'd never sold any," Elaine continued. "Apparently they needed someone to make them for the Market, and she wondered if I would consider doing that. I was willing to try, and the first day we were here I sold $50 worth of cakes. I couldn't believe it! It was unreal to me. I was floored when Marie Blackwell, a preacher's wife from Dana Baptist, told me to sell each half a cake for $5.00. She used to work at the jelly tables and was such a help to me, but I was amazed at the price she suggested. I was really tickled when everything sold! I went home so thrilled that day. The Lord truly has had a hand in this, because my pound cakes have become a wonderful business. I make 15 different varieties from the same basic recipe: almond, lemon, butter pecan, and all the flavors you can imagine. With rising costs, my cakes sell for a little more now, but with the baking I do on Mondays, Wednesdays and Fridays they're always fresh for the Curb."

Picking up her story again, Elaine said, "Along with the cakes, Stanley's woodworking, and other items we sold back then, I was also filling in whenever our manager, Dan Volkert, took some time off. One Tuesday morning in 2001, he didn't show up for work. He had died from a heart attack, which was especially sad because he was only 53, and everyone liked Dan. At that time, I became the fulltime manager."

Dan accepted the manager's position in May, 1994. He knew well the workings of the Market, having been involved since 1955 when his parents, Herbert and Doris Cooke Volkert, became members. Doris had actually started at the Curb 15 years earlier when she began helping her Uncle Frank and Aunt Jessie Bradbury sell both the wooden items Frank made and the dahlias Jessie grew. Later, the Volkerts had a similar business, and Dan was at the same table selling his burned wooden plaques, a process known as pyrography. Doris served on the Board of Control from 1981 until 1997. Their daughter, Pam Volkert Lewis, later inherited one of their tables.

"I enjoy my position as manager," Elaine continued, "but it took me a while to adjust to several things. At first I wouldn't use the intercom because I didn't like the way my voice sounded over the loud speaker; instead I'd walk to a booth if I needed to talk with someone. I finally got tired of doing that. Several years ago I started on the radio, WTZQ AM 1600. Every Saturday morning I talk with Hollywood (Frank "Hollywood" Jones) and tell him what's going on at the Curb Market, the type of seasonal produce that's available, if there's a book signing, and anything else to encourage the listeners to come down to the Curb. I was very nervous when I first started, but Hollywood had a tip for me. He told me not to think of it as being on the radio, but like we were talking together on the telephone. That helped."

Elaine has a fascinating personal heritage that fits well in the Scots-Irish ancestral soil of Western North Carolina. Her father, Duncan McCauley Duncan, was a young man when he left Scotland for America to become a textile engraver. After a number of years in Norwich, Connecticut, he brought his family and skills to Henderson County where he continued his work in the textile industry. The year was 1958, and Elaine was 10 years old.

An important story exists about her father. "Before the start of World War II, Daddy and two other men worked on a top-secret, government project to create a fabric pattern that would blend into the ground, something to replace the solid, drab olive-green. I understand they created several patterns, laid them on the ground outside, and then flew over in an airplane to see which ones blended in the best. According to my brother Bob, they contributed to the development of the camouflage used by our military. My dad, typical of that generation, was very modest, and for the longest time we didn't know anything about his involvement. Our mother finally told us."

Once in Hendersonville, her family took to the community, enjoying their new life in the Blue Ridge. The mid-1960s soon rolled around, and Elaine has much to recall about this town and the teen traditions reflective of that era. "I met Stanley in 1966, when I was 17 and he was 22. I first saw him at the Skyline Drive-in on Greenville Highway, one of the popular hangout spots. We used to go there to eat after cruising Main Street, which was wide and straight back then. Sometimes, we'd go across the street to Brock's Drive-in, another popular place to eat. One day when I was at Skyline, I saw this nice-looking guy drive through - and I was interested! Turns out my brother knew him. We soon met and started dating, and Stanley and I were married in 1967. We have three great children, Gail, Michael and Deborah, as well as four wonderful grandsons."

Before the morning ended, I visited Stanley's booth to see his beautiful woodwork. His shelves were lined with fascinating, collapsible baskets in a variety of intriguing shapes. There were baskets shaped like apples, teapots, tulips and one that said 'Country Welcome' - each one stunning and a compliment to his wide assortment of wood products.

"I like to make all kinds of things, whatever I want to do," Stanley said, and with all he was selling, he truly does. "I'm a retired brick mason after 40 years and fortunate to still be working and able to have a table here at the Curb. This is an interesting place, because I get to meet and talk with a lot of different types of people, and some people really like to talk! It's just a neat place to be."

Stanley is a vendor at the Market, but he holds another position, too. He's the "Gravy Maker" for the spring and fall "Ol' Timey Days" celebrations, cooking his sausage gravy on a wood-fired cook stove, reminiscent of the olden days. Spooned over hot country biscuits, this comfort food is true southern fare.

I stopped by the manager's desk to pick up my cake before I left and to thank Elaine again for taking time to share her story with me. She echoed the sentiments I hear so often from others, "I love the Curb Market. I used to come by, but I never dreamed I'd be here, let alone become the manager. I love the traditions and hope the Curb keeps going for years to come."

Oh, I couldn't agree more!

Several months after our interview, the Staton family experienced a life-changing, deeply sorrowful event when Stanley died from an aneurism on May 24, 2009 at age 65. This respected Curb Market vendor, Ralph Stanley Staton, was a life-long resident of Henderson County, the son of the late Frank and Hattie Lytle Staton.

Our prayers are with Elaine and the family. Stanley will be sorely missed.

Chapter Nine
Flowers: Dried, Arranged, Inviting
Larry & Nancy Justice Ball
A Third Generation Vendor

Nancy Ball
(Photo by Ann Wirtz)

"What kind of plant is this?" I asked Nancy Justice Ball one Saturday in early December. I wanted greenery to combine with a Christmas ribbon to attach to my outdoor lamppost, something with berries and a fullness which would underscore the lantern. I had stopped at the Curb Market's southwest corner booth, one that overwhelms the visual sense with its colorful variety and enormity of selection. I knew the booth belonged to Larry and Nancy Justice Ball, and they would undoubtedly have what I was looking for.

Whenever I passed by, I would find their multiple tables eye-catching with up-side-down bouquets of dried flowers, branches of pussy willows and the paper-thin money plant. I would always admire the hydrangea flowers of multiple hues and the neutral grasses, knowing how lovely they'd be in any decorating scheme. I have observed that whatever the time of year, they always have something to perfectly represent the season.

On this particular morning, I was again drawn to Nancy's corner where she identified the branch I'd chosen, "That's Nandina; it lasts well. It's a variety that grows as a tall bush, the kind often seen around older homes. If you leave it outside, the birds will eventually eat the berries; inside it'll last longer." The Nandina, also known as "heavenly bamboo," made a perfect choice, still a satisfying sight well into January.

I came back again to talk with Nancy, curious about her heritage as a third-generation, Curb Market vendor. As she tells it, she was practically born at the Curb. The year was 1940, and she was a month old when her Uncle Raymond and Aunt Daisy Justice Pace brought her with them as they worked their Curb Market booth. They placed her in the paper box, which held newspapers to wrap the flowers they sold. Nancy has been a regular at the Market ever since.

The Paces had a farm on Ridge Road in Dana, across from Nancy's parents, B.P. (Ben) and Helen Youngblood Justice. "Aunt Daisy and Uncle Raymond never had children, so I was like their daughter, and they were like parents to me. My grandparents, Ben and Nancy Ann Hyder Justice, also farmed up the road from us. They, too, were like another set of parents, so if I wasn't home I was either with one family or the other. My grandfather was a wonderful man, who had so much love to give everyone.

"My grandparents, Mamaw and Papaw (Nancy Ann and Ben) were vendors from the start. For years they supplied produce from their farm to the boarding houses in town, delivering by horse and wagon. The idea of a central place where people would come to them instead was very appealing."

Nancy continued, "Their daughter, my Aunt Daisy, was a young girl that first day on Main Street, and she baked a cake to sell. She was always with her parents, selling her cakes. Daisy's sister, Effie Justice Allen, became famous for her laurel baskets filled with mosses, berries and woodland plants. The tourists from Charleston or Florida would buy them in order to take a little bit of the mountains back home. Effie eventually became a stockholder and maintained a booth for 20 years."

Another Curb family connection is Knox and Altha Willis Hyder. Knox was Nancy Ann's brother. The "book of memories" states Altha was the first to make the upside-down dolls which became so popular. Her dolls added to the produce, fruit, and flowers they sold.

Conversation flowed the morning we talked, as Nancy Ball had nearly 70 years of personal Curb Market memories to recall. "When I was old enough to comprehend my surroundings, I remember crowds of people and noise, lots of noise! It was difficult to walk up to the office to get change for the booth, which I often did; it was like walking through a gauntlet with people crowding on both sides.

"When the stock holders bought this property, it was an old wood yard, where lumber and wood were sold to heat homes. They constructed a wooden building to house the Curb Market, replacing it in 1955 with the brick building we have now. Originally, there were huge pot belly stoves up the center, where the men would congregate to talk and chew tobacco. We even had a front porch on the first building, where my dad sold little puppies, probably beagles. Kittens were there, too."

Nancy Ball's World of Flowers
(Photo by Ann Wirtz)

Nancy gestured, "Inside, near our booth, running across the middle, there was a wooden meat counter with a glass front; it had a sliding door, and ice would be put in the bottom to keep it cold. A person would sign up to sell meat on a particular day, often pork, sliced ham, homemade sausage, or beef. Chickens were usually dressed and displayed in a dish pan at individual booths. Sometimes there'd be fresh rabbit. If someone was only selling a ham slice at the meat counter, they'd pay me 10 or 25 cents to sell for them. It was a way I could make some money, and they didn't have to mess with the meat."

Nancy's grandparents were notably successful selling a variety of items at the Curb, two items in particular. "My grandmother made cottage cheese in the smoke house, where she'd strain it till it was a lump of white cheese," Nancy said. "She'd add fresh, thick cream, a little salt, and I can still taste it today! People loved it. My grandparents were also famous for their country cured ham.

"I remember we brought flowers, vegetables, and apples to sell. We grew a lot of spinach. Mr. Reuben from Osceola Lake Inn would buy bushels of spinach to use at the inn. When we went to the Curb Market, we'd take out the back car seat and load the car with all our items, putting the spinach on the running board and vegetables on the fenders. We'd get in, and it was quite a sight!

"Daisy and Raymond started the flowers," Nancy said. "They made extensive gardens, where the perennials and annuals still grow. In season, we cut every day and process them in an old log building. We have both a retail and wholesale business. Daisy was very talented and loved to make dried flower arrangements. At Christmas, Uncle Raymond would make wreaths using all natural plants like Boxwood, Arbor Vitae, Holly, and cones. He'd make wreaths for the courthouse and City Hall. My son, Shannon, and his wife, Robbie, still make the wreaths the same way to sell for the holidays."

Nancy and Larry have two sons, Shannon and Shane, who are 4th generation vendors; they each have a table at the Curb. Another son, Darien, works with the flowers at the Biltmore Estate in Asheville, carrying on the knowledge and tradition he inherited. Granddaughters Katie and Erinn starting selling at the Curb Market when they were each 10 years old, making them 5th generation vendors. They make angels out of lace. According to Nancy, their brother Eli, when he was young, would collect "little-boy stuff" to sell, like birds' nests and other treasures.

It's easy to admire the longevity and creative contribution this family has made to the Curb Market. With the beauty and industry of their work on display, I shouldn't have been astonished by another discovery. Larry, who was on the Board of Control for 20 years, fashions hornets' nests into everything from small animals to lampshades and large baskets. One especially beautiful basket has deer antlers for its handle. A gentleman stopped when I was there, his eyes scanning Larry's work, and commented in amazement, "I never would have thought you could make anything like this from a hornet's nest!" Exactly.

As we wound up our time together, Nancy observed, "There have always been a lot of personalities at the Curb Market. Growing up here, we were like a family, and we learned how to get along, working around our differences. Back then, we knew each other, knew the families well. That's harder today."

Nancy concluded softly, "This is my home; I treat it like my home. I worry about this place when I'm not here. You see, this is my life. I'm not just here; I live it."

The Henderson County Curb Market history is about the people of the Blue Ridge, about North Carolina families and genealogy. New vendors who hail from near or far are welcomed today for their contribution to the continuing success of the Market, but the "ol' timey" families with their many decades of commitment are revered for their legacy. They're part of a priceless heritage.

Nancy's lifetime impact on the Curb Market and on our understanding of its valuable history can never be overstated. When illness kept her from her appointed spot in the southwest corner of the Market, she was greatly missed. Every visit I made to the Curb had always included a few minutes of conversation with this legendary woman. Sadly, Nancy died on May 11, 2010. Our sincere condolences and prayers are offered to the family; may they know their devastating loss is felt by the friends and customers Nancy faithfully served. She will never be forgotten.

Chapter Ten
The Wildflower Lady and Her Cousins
Louise Jackson Hill and the King Family
Knowledge and Beauty to Share

Louise Hill
(Photo by Ann Wirtz)

    The first item I ever bought from Louise Hill was a gumdrop tree. It was Christmastime, and I was walking the aisles of the Curb Market with hot cider in hand, taking in the festivities, loving the bustle of activity. Drawn as I am to colors, textures and images that are wholesome and inspiring, I immediately stopped in front of her gumdrop trees, awash in memories.

    For as many years as I can remember a small, clear plastic tree materialized every December on the living room bookcase of my girlhood home. It was adorned with gumdrops of every hue, which always captured my fancy. Nothing has changed! My fancy was caught again, and thoughts of my mother, and Christmas, and childhood compelled me to purchase a tree for my own home.

    Louise's trees are different, however. They're actually made from a wild

Crab Apple branch, its spikes vibrant with gumdrops. Anchored in a red pot with stiffened foam for support, the tree makes a lovely table centerpiece. I positioned my small nativity set on both sides of my gumdrop tree with Mary, Joseph, Baby Jesus and the sheep balancing the cattle, donkey and watering trough.

Govan and Mintie King
(Photo courtesy of the Curb Market)

This is what a stroll through the Curb Market does. It connects us with memories, provides beauty for our lives, and feeds our souls with joy. It's also an educational experience, for the next time I visited Louise, I received a nature lesson. It was graciously taught and eagerly received by both myself and a young man who was in town to see his grandfather. Chris Hoffman, at the time an eighth grader from Norfolk, Virginia, was as intrigued as I was with Louise's offerings.

I was absorbed by the range of her items: pussy willows, a hornet's nest of immense proportions that was formed on her deck window, a terrarium, and various birds' nests including a tiny hummingbird nest made from moss and lichen and no doubt lined with plant down and spider-webs.

As I studied her extensive assortment, Louise presented a box containing a snake skin, translucent and paper-thin. She said softly, "I only pull this out to show if I think someone would be interested in seeing it. I enjoy educating the children. They're usually the most fascinated with all this."

A few minutes later, Chris stopped to admire the hornet's nest, which Louise explained was made from the plentiful poplar wood. As a hornet chews on wood fibers, the fibers mix with the hornet's saliva. The mixture is then deposited in gray, papery layers to form a nest substantial enough to withstand any kind of weather.

"Would you like to see a snake skin?" Louise asked, as she again pulled her box from beneath the counter, sure of Chris' response. "This is a whole skin from a nonpoisonous snake, probably a garter snake. I remember my dad killing a poisonous snake once, and when it was opened up, 22 little snakes were still alive in its mouth. We think they went there in response to the danger. Nonpoisonous snakes usually lay eggs, but most poisonous snakes birth live babies (which have hatched from eggs within the mother)." We knew nothing about snakes, or had long forgotten, and were awed by the intricacies

The Henderson County Curb Market 49

of snake life which Louise shared with us that morning.

Chris eventually wandered on, vowing to be back when he visited again. Louise smiled and said, "That's what I like about young people. They're interested in what I have and are appreciative."

For young or old, visiting Louise is always a treat; her knowledge and friendliness fun to be around. As a primary vendor for more than 30 years, Louise considers the people her source of pleasure. "I enjoy the Curb Market, meeting friends, associating with them, getting to know new people," she explained.

Louise grew up here, helping to sell produce from her parent's farm. Her mother and father, Dudley and Essie King Jackson, *"were among the first sellers of the Curb Market,"* and in the 1999 "book of memories," their commitment to the Market is remembered. *"They made their move with the market each time it was relocated. In September of 1972, Dudley suffered a massive heart attack and went to be with his Lord while serving his customers from his market table. After the death of Dudley Jackson, Essie continued to sell at the Curb Market for an additional 26 years...She was well known for the delicious jams, jellies, fruit pies, and her red raspberries. She had a great love for nature and her wildflowers and enjoyed sharing them with her customers. Essie also brought...home grown eggs and her pieced quilts...Mrs. Jackson passed away on July 30, 1998, only about a month after bad health forced her retirement at the age of only 93."*

Dudley and Essie had 13 children, and Louise was the fifth child. "We were born and raised in Upward, but I've lived on Sugarloaf Road in the Edneyville/Dana area for over 50 years now," Louise shared. "Daddy was a raspberry farmer, which paid for the college education of those in the family who went. He also raised apples. He was a good manager, and I remember he once had 35 pickers working at one time."

Louise's grandparents were Govan and Arminta "Mintie" Case King from Upward, and they, too, sold farm produce from their Curb Market booth, beginning when the Curb was first located on Main Street. According to the "book of memories," the Kings would spend *"a long hot day in the fields harvesting vegetables and fruit for the Curb Market...Being a seller on the 'Curb' required this couple to rise in the very early morning to make it into town in time to meet their customers with their goods in their horse drawn wagon."*

"My parents and grandparents worked very hard," Louise stated. "That was their way of life, but it's our way of life, too. All the family is involved at the Curb, from my husband of 59 years (in 2009), Harvey DeWitt Hill, to our children and grandchildren. Harvey works mostly in the garden preparing the produce we sell. His specialty is home-grown tomatoes. Our son Edsel has this table next to mine, where he sells vegetables in the spring and summer.

His wife Lugenia makes these hand-towels. Edsel would be a fourth generation vendor, and my grandchildren who also come in would be fifth-generation sellers. Our daughter Etrula, 'Trudy,' is either working in the booth with me or helping other vendors."

Trudy indeed steps in when there's a need. "I was brought up to lend a helping hand" is her simple, matter-of-fact explanation. She was working at her friend's table the day we chatted, Tom Hollifield, his garden vegetables on fine display. Trudy speaks for her family, and for many others, when she describes membership at the Curb as "part of a great tradition."

Louise has several cousins who have tables at the Market: Ralph and Lucy Stepp King and their daughter Cindy Hudgins. Also, Ralph's brother Charlie and his wife Gladys Wilson King sell produce fresh from their garden. The brothers have always been part of the Curb. "I was raised here," Ralph exclaimed, and Charlie once said he'd been at the Market since he "was knee high to a duck."

Their grandparents were involved from the beginning, Will and Lama Edney Jackson and Govan and Mintie King, as well as their parents, Albert and Dorothy Jackson King. Ralph, who has been chairman of the Board of Control several times, recalled one morning, "Our parents sold produce and fresh meat, which you could back then. I enjoyed coming to the Curb; it got me out of plowing and hoeing back home!"

Ralph's family started cultivating flowers for the Market in 1964, and now many a landscaped lawn boasts their day lilies, hostas, and hydrangea. Daughter Cindy has her own business at the Curb called "A Touch of the Mountains." She specializes in "occasions on a budget" using fresh and dried flowers, along with the magnificent hydrangeas which lend themselves beautifully to arrangements, even wreaths, which I'd never seen done before.

Wreaths enliven Cindy's booth, creating a virtual feast for the eyes. Hers are a stunning, seasonal assortment: wreaths made from pussy willows, forever the harbingers of spring; the summer hydrangea, elegant in form and color; and in the fall of the year the coveted bittersweet. Ah, bittersweet. Another memory tug, as every autumn my mom always had a sprig in a small brass vase on that same bookcase that would sport the gumdrop tree in December. Every year I buy my own bittersweet, continuing the tradition that takes me back to Webster Groves, Missouri, and those treasured growing up years. I bought some from Cindy; others sell it as well. Our fireplace mantle held the bittersweet this year, a bright loveliness running the length of the wood and accenting autumn candles and memento. It made a pleasing sight.

The satisfaction received from the Market's offerings is only surpassed by the Market's distinctive history; it's all about family. Not everyone is related anymore, but the ol' time family surnames that helped settle this community are still present here: the Kings, the Jacksons, the Hills, the...well, the list is long, and many of the early county names would be found on the earliest Curb membership lists, if they existed.

As time passes, age and circumstance cause individuals to leave the Market. Sometimes children and relatives, for various reasons, decline to continue the family's membership. Ruth Esther Reed Ooley is one who fits this category. She was pleased to share a bit of her family's story one day. "My mother is kin to the King clan, Marie King Reed."

Marie is the daughter of William Alonzo and Anne Esther Garren King. In genealogy speak, William Alonzo and Govan King are first cousins twice removed. Marie married a gentleman from Ohio, Allen Edgar Reed, and apparently made quite a stir. "Everyone thought she was crazy to marry a Yankee," Ruth confided. "Some didn't understand that. My parents were some of the original Curb Market members. They had a truck farm, a small field and garden where we'd work until dark getting produce ready to sell. When grubbing dirt got to be too hard, my mother started sewing for the Curb. She was a very good seamstress, each stitch carefully made.

"I was only 8 or 9, a little girl," Ruth recalled thoughtfully, "and I remember feeling proud and honored to be at the Curb. My job was to make change for the customers." She concluded, "My sister Jennie Reed Warren had a table for a while, but no one is at the Curb from my family now. I grew up there; I liked it. There was a clannish air, no scandals; people lived a straight life, as I remember it."

This chapter began with Louise and took some turns, as family stories and connections do. It will end, however, with her final thoughts. "My true hobby is raising flowers," Louise said simply. "I inherited my mother's love for nature, and I enjoy sharing that at the Curb. Plants live on, and we can enjoy them. We'd never know what certain ones looked like if we didn't keep them growing." Spoken like a true daughter, or son, of the King family!

As you stop at Louise's booth, you'll find her warm smile and respectful ways a benediction over the array of natural items that enhance her northeast corner tables. As she gently imparts her experience and knowledge, we are the better for knowing her.

Chapter Eleven
From the Beginning
Pat Walker
Remembering the Past

Callie and Pat Walker
(Photo courtesy of the Curb Market)

"I grew up here. I remember how it used to be," Pat said softly. "All the older people are gone now. I miss my mom, my aunts, and all the other ladies who made a difference. There were many couples at the Curb Market over the years who truck farmed; that's how they made their living. They're gone." Pat Walker, a third-generation vendor, described the reality of time passing, a generational passing which brings tears to the eyes as loved ones are remembered.

"My mom was Callie Case Walker," Pat said proudly. "She was with the Curb Market from the beginning. She sold on Main Street the first day and went to King Street and then on to Church Street and was here until her death in 1996. She was active in the Curb for more than 70 years. Callie originally sold cakes, and later she and my dad, Grady Walker, sold vegetables and fresh flowers.

"They'd grow dahlias, zinnias, snapdragons, and baby's breath, to name some. They had plants like pansies, other perennials and annuals, too," Pat said. "When that got to be too much, they switched to dried flowers and did arrangements. They would pick plants that grow wild to use as fillers, plants like rabbit tobacco and pepper grass, which were dried and spray-painted."

Pat's grandparents, Andrew P. and Ella Jay Hyder Case, lived on Sugarloaf Road in the Dana area, where they also raised vegetables and flowers to sell.

In the "book of memories," which Pat and her cousin Terry Robinson compiled, she wrote, *"Ella Jay sold at the Market...and many of the ladies from the boarding houses in Hendersonville would buy from her."*

Pat explained, "In those days, there were a lot of boarding houses behind us on 5th Avenue. They'd prepare three meals a day, so this was a convenient place for them to buy the food they needed. They would also buy flowers. Of course, the boarding houses are long gone, but they provided important customers for the Curb back then. So did the summer camps for kids located in Tuxedo and on Lake Osceola; we sold a lot of food to them."

All of Ella Jay and Andrew's four daughters were involved in some way with the Curb: Callie, Madolen, Marie and Vena. Marie was a school teacher, so her contribution was primarily to drive her mother and Madolen to the Market, as neither of them ever learned how to drive. Marie's driving skills averted a crisis one day, which Pat indirectly acknowledged in the "book of memories."

"(Ella Jay) was cleaning her table. The money she had made that day was put in the trash and taken to the incinerator on Seventh Avenue. She and Marie followed the trash truck. When the men were dumping the trash, a wet paper bag with the money came open and the money was found – that was a lucky day." Indeed!

Madolen was especially active at the Curb, and Pat laughingly shared, "She never married, which kind of runs in the family. She helped her mother when the Market was on King Street and then here. After Ella died, Madolen inherited her table. She continued selling flowers, using dried flowers to decorate fans and brooms, as well as for traditional arrangements. When Madolen passed, the table was issued to her nephew Terry Robinson, who was Vena's son."

Vena Case Robinson sold handcrafts and crocheted afghans, along with church dolls made from a handkerchief or from a piece of square fabric. Pat had her own basket of church dolls, and I was quite taken with them and the history they represented. A card was attached to each doll stating, *"I am a 'Church Doll.' Years ago, such dolls were made to be played with during church services. They became 'special' since playing with them was limited to those hours."* I could just envision a little girl captivated by her doll, naming it perhaps Charlotte or Emma, a delightful companion to make the time pass more quickly.

When she saw my enthusiasm, Pat generously said, "I want you to pick out a couple." So I gladly did, choosing two for my toy collection. According to Historical Folk Toys in Nashville, Indiana, handkerchief dolls were made for little girls to carry to church, a practice especially popular during the Civil

War era. These "Sunday toys" were noiseless and provided an amusing distraction. The handkerchief doll has been given a variety of names over the years: a church, pew, or prayer doll, and a church or pew baby. Oh, the ingenuity of that first mother who quickly formed a doll with her hankie to still her restless daughter...a whimsical notion with a satisfactory outcome.

Satisfying, too, is the remembrance of her family's Curb Market history, which Pat was delighted to discuss. "My own earliest memories are of being a little bitty gal running around and playing with the other kids," Pat said. "I remember the crowds of people, too, and it seems like we were a lot busier then. Folks from Florida who came regularly to their summer homes in the mountains always came to the Curb, and now their children and grandchildren carry on that tradition."

Pat continued, "I recall the stoves that went up the center that were used to heat the building. I know our table has always been in this same location (the northwest aisle, across from the side door). My brother, Grady Walker Jr., used to work at home helping prepare the vegetables and flowers we'd bring here to sell. When my dad died in 1978, my mom continued for almost another 20 years. She did a lot of crocheting, made quilted pillows, and she started making the beaded bandanas, all which I still sell."

As our conversation came to a close, Pat gestured to the painting hanging on the wall near the rear entrance and said, "My mom is in that picture." We walked over to admire the early Curb Market scene, the original photograph now captured for all time by artist RuthEllen Boerman. The picture graces the cover of the booklet Pat and Terry compiled to commemorate *"75 years of memories."*

A description of the photograph is included in the article written by Linda March for the April, 1994 issue of the Blue Ridge Business Journal. *"This photo shows three enterprising young women, each part of the original 4-H group. Mrs. (Callie) Walker, just 17 then, in the white-collared dress...had a cake that day. 'And I sold it,' she remembers proudly."*

After Callie died, Pat inherited her mother's table, continuing the tradition started almost a century ago. The longevity of the Curb Market and its generational history is astonishing to contemplate; especially when it seems just yesterday when loved ones were here.

Chapter Twelve
World-renowned Artist and Author
Ruth Ellen Connell Boerman
A Woman of Faith

RuthEllen Boerman
(Photo by Ann Wirtz)

"I never knew I had any talent," RuthEllen Connell Busbee Boerman shared one spring morning as we sat in her art studio and gallery in her Hendersonville home.

This statement was remarkable, considering the paintings that adorned her walls were each a masterpiece of inspiration and beauty: mountains and valleys, flowers and trees, birds and sheep – all her glorious work.

"Mother always had art materials around, so we drew all the time. She had artistic talent, but she never developed her skills; instead she devoted herself to raising her five children. My father was an engineer with that kind of technical, draftsman ability. Besides the opportunities at home, I remember drawing a lot in school, which is probably why my grades weren't any good!" she laughed.

"A teacher once asked me to draw an apple tree for the bulletin board after she saw some of my sketches, but I was hesitant, not sure she meant it. By the time I finally decided she really wanted me to do this, I came into class and noticed an apple tree had already been drawn and put up by another student. I took it personally back then, deciding I really wasn't any good, that the teacher really hadn't meant it when she asked me to do the drawing. It wasn't until I was a mother in the early 1980s helping my son, Tim, with an art project for school that I began to realize I might have some talent. I had actually painted a picture for my mother about 10 years earlier, but I considered that just a fluke."

RuthEllen described the turning point in her life that led to that painting. "After a childhood in Saratoga, New York, and Virginia, I got involved with the wrong people during my teen years in Hendersonville. I made some poor choices, and finally when I was in my 20s, I remembered my mother's faith and the God she had always talked about. I called to Him and asked Him to change my life, and He did."

She moved back into her mother's home and was inspired to paint a mountain scene with a trail and a woman with her hands open, her arms outstretched. Along the bottom of the painting RuthEllen wrote, "O magnify the Lord with me, and let us exalt His name together," from Psalm 34:3.

"About this same time," RuthEllen continued, "I got reacquainted with Jeff Busbee at the church we were attending. We had known each other in high school in the early 60s. We were married in 1972 and had two children, Tim and Andrea. I wanted to be home with them, so I prayed about ways I could supplement our income. Art and Craft Fairs seemed to be the answer, so I painted nature scenes on saws, skillets, mailboxes, even slices of wood, and they sold very well. We did this from 1982 to 1989."

After five years, RuthEllen was burned out from the fair circuit and contemplated other ways to market her art work. Jeff was working with Larry Ball at G.E. and knew the Ball family was involved at the Curb Market. Fortunately, Larry was able to help them get a booth as day renters during the week. Eventually, they were assigned their own table.

"That's how the Lord got me out of doing craft shows!" RuthEllen exclaimed. "Interestingly, along the way I started receiving comments that changed the direction of my painting. People were suggesting I do 'fine art,' that my talent was 'more worthy' than (showcasing it) on saws. This was an encouragement to me, which led to the pastoral paintings.

"I love the Curb Market, and during the approximately 11 years we were here, we had such a great time meeting people, both vendors and customers. I developed quite a following, especially with my inspirational paintings," RuthEllen said.

She talked about painting the famous Curb Market scene titled "First Curb Market Days," which was unveiled and given to the Market for its 65th Anniversary celebration in 1989. RuthEllen recalled, "I was asked to do the painting from an old black and white photo. Callie Walker was one of the young women in the picture, and it was fun to talk with her about the early days of the Curb Market and to capture that particular memory on canvas. It took me back to that era." With a wistful smile she added, "I'm basically an old-fashioned person. I should have lived back then, even the late 1800s." Ah, those words resonated within me. I could tell this woman and I would become good friends.

Several years after this painting was completed, RuthEllen's focus took another turn. She revealed, "I went through a difficult, emotionally low period of time, but out of that came the inspiration to paint what has become my best seller to date, 'The True Vine.' The success of this painting confirmed the direction I had started to take with my art work, and I named my business True Vine Studio. In 1997, a print of this painting was presented to South Carolina's past governor, David Beasley."

She continued her story, "Jeff and I worked together at the Curb Market, where he was asked to serve on the Board of Directors. He was well liked, which made his death in July, 1998, especially difficult. He had gone through minor surgery, and no one picked up on a blood clot that formed.

"After the shock of his death, I eventually headed in another direction. I finished at the Curb Market and began going on mission trips with First Baptist, my home church. I've been to Russia four times, spending six weeks in St. Petersburg in 2002. These trips were opportunities to serve in orphanages, churches and camps, as well as to lead ladies' Bible study groups. I loved meeting the wonderful Russian people and seeing their beautiful land. I also went to Israel during this time, another amazing country."

The year before RuthEllen went to St. Petersburg she served on another outreach committee at church and met her second husband, Joe Boerman. He was also widowed, and they "hit it off immediately," RuthEllen proclaimed. They were married in September, 2002. "Joe is a great encourager of my art work and business, and we love to travel together." They had just returned from a trip to Israel when we met for this interview.

In 1996, RuthEllen began a series of paintings on the 23rd Psalm. She completed several canvases, but with her first husband's death and the many changes and challenges from that sorrow, little progress was made in completing her work. In January, 2004, Joe asked about her business plan for the year, and her inspired reply was to finish what she'd begun eight years earlier. By June, all ten paintings were completed.

RuthEllen has written, "The paintings (portraying the 23rd Psalm) depict the life of sheep in various times and seasons. Some contain a waterfall or a night scene with a moon shining brightly, a spectacular sunset, fabulous mountain views, a faithful sheep dog, and the shepherd. Each piece has the popular hidden objects (the paintings) are noted for that tie in with Biblical and inspirational concepts." This series and all her paintings are reproduced by the Giclee printing method, chosen because each canvas reproduction has the appearance of the original painting and can be hand embellished.

Her stunning work is fortunately available at the Curb Market. Her paintings can also be purchased at The Open Door Christian Bookstore located at Hendersonville's Blue Ridge Mall. A number of stores in the area carry her book, *My Favorite Psalm*, a 2006 release featuring RuthEllen's paintings on the 23rd Psalm and her inspirational description of each picture. One of her paintings in this series titled, "He Makes Me Lie Down in Green Pastures," graced the cover of the Spring 2008 quarterly magazine, "Safe Home," published by the Little Sisters of the Poor, a charity in London, England. In 2006, RuthEllen's patriotic painting, "One Nation Under God," was given by the Presidential Prayer Team organization to President George W. Bush in honor of his birthday. Her artwork literally spans the world's capitals!

"I see my work and my talent as a gift from God," RuthEllen explained humbly, as she shared the multiple ways her inspirational artwork has been recognized. "I want to encourage women from all walks of life to develop their talents and to persevere in spite of difficulties."

After our time together, RuthEllen and Joe made the exciting decision for her to return to the Curb Market. "I missed the people," she said simply. "I love the sense of community and family we have here. This is a wonderful place to sell my artwork and to connect with everyday people. I think I was craving what this place represents, and the Lord led me back."

RuthEllen's artwork was again honored in 2009 when her delicate watercolor of a full and branching apple tree was chosen as the logo for the 63rd Annual North Carolina Apple Festival, a Labor Day weekend tradition in Hendersonville. Her painting was inspired by the verse in John 15:16, "You did not choose Me, but I chose you and appointed you to go and bear fruit – fruit that will last." Her grade school experience came full circle with the selection of her apple tree, a painting from the heart of her faith.

Chapter Thirteen
Pickles and Chutney ~ Joyce Hill Pace
Still a Vendor at 95

Joyce Pace sells pickles to Lou Reeves
(Photo by Ann Wirtz)

"Cain I help y'all with somethin'?" Joyce asked the man as he held up a jar of her pickles. "If y'd like a good pickle," Joyce said knowingly, "y'll like these. Y' come back, an' I'll fix y' up." The man came back and bought two jars of dill pickles and a jar each of pickled green beans and squash.

Friendly and still determined to make a sale at age 95, Joyce Pace explained, "I use my own recipe; it varies some d'pendin' on what I'm cannin'." The jar labels say basically the same thing:

The Name of the Product
Weight – 16 oz
$4.50
Mrs. Herbert J. Pace
Hendersonville, NC   Route 6
Contents: Vinegar, Sugar, Onions, Peppers, Spices.

Her combinations lead to a nice selection for the buyer:
Bread and Butter Pickles – "m' #1 sell'r"
Dill Pickles – "m' fav'rit"
Chutney – "appl' an' peach an' d'licious with meats"
Artichoke Pickles
Artichoke Relish – "both mild an' hot"
Squash Pickles
Pickled Okra
Pickled Beans
Chow-Chow

"I made cakes when I first started, 12 kinds of pound cake: s'r cream, but'rnut, choc'late, almond, an' I cain't 'memb'r 'em all. They were my original recipes an' I won many first an' second place ribb'ns at the fair. In 19-an'-62, I won both first an' second on my cakes," Joyce explained proudly.

"I got tired of makin' 'em one day," Joyce said, "an' d'cided it was time to start doin' somethin' else. That was in 1996. I put my pans away an' haven't made a cake since."

Joyce is a second generation vendor, inheriting her table from her father, Leander "Lee" Hill. "My mother was Fidelia Blanche Osteen Hill an' my father started bringin' her to the Curb Market in 1928 when hit was still on King Street. She sold chick'ns, veg'tables, but'r, but'rmilk, eggs an' berries, ev'n cakes in 'er last years. Aft'r droppin' 'er off, Daddy'd go back home to work, then come back to pick 'er up.

"When I was big enough, Daddy wanted me to bring 'er, but I was afraid of learnin' to drive. In 19-an'-40, I d'cided I didn't want to have to walk ev'rtime I wanted to go some place, or have to ask someone to take me. I learnt to drive, an' in all these years, I've nev'r had a speedin' ticket, not ev'n an accident. That's a record! I'd be lost if I didn't drive!

"I drove my mother to Market an' helped 'er when she was busy an' needed me; then she passed away in 1953. Daddy gave me 'er booth in '54, an' I've been comin' ev'r since, back then comin' year round.

"I was born on Ju-ly 5th, 1912, an' raised in Dana on my parent's farm. I married my husband, Herbert J. Pace, in 19-an'-36. We had a big appl' orchard; an' Herbert was a good gardn'r, raisin' veg'tables which he'd wash an' get ready to sell here. He passed in '96. My son, Wayne, op'rates the orchard now, on Appl' Blossom Lane.

"I 'tribute my health to three things: I don't smoke, don't drink; don't use drugs. I had a heart attack in April of '92. When I had a physical this year, the doct'r said, 'You know, Joyce, hit's remarkable the kind of health you have now, an' how you've recov'r'd.' Cain't hear, tho'; cain't help with that.

"I try to eat right an' sensible. I once weighed 175 lbs," she smiled, knowing I'd find that hard to believe, which I did, slender as she is. "I became a bord'rline diabetic an' had to watch my sug'r intake, so I lost weight.

"I have two sons almost within hollerin' distance of me, Vincent Lee and Herbert Wayne. They're always lookin' aft'r me. I live on Ridge Road, in front of the Dana School.

"My husband, Herbert, was 6 years old'r than me. When I asked him why he took so long to propose, he always said he had to wait for me to grow up! We were raised in the same church, Refuge Baptist, but I've been at Dana Baptist now for a long time. We had three boys, the youngest, Larry Dean, died from cancer. I have five gran'children, one is deceased, an' four great gran'children.

"I'm kind of tired of talkin' now," this precious lady politely informed me. Besides, more customers were coming to her booth to look over her selection, and we didn't want her to miss a sale!

"This is my last Sat'rday 'til spring," she added. "In the winter, hit's too cold to come in."

We'll miss you, Joyce; we'll look forward to your return.

And return she occasionally did, surprisingly, even before the warmth of April. There was always a minute to stop for a hug and a brief chat, and I had the opportunity to share this chapter; which she approved, dialect and all.

"P'll out that chair and set a bit," she'd say. "How're y' doin?" And with that, we'd share an update on our lives.

A bit later, I stopped in the Market before Mother's Day to pick up the caramel cake I'd ordered from Marilyn Horne. Joyce was already here several booths down, her radiant countenance drawing me in for that dear hug. Her pretty face and capable manner belied her 95 years.

As we talked, I studied the jellies on the counter, and the sunlight seemed to illuminate the claret red of one particular jar. "What kind of jelly is that?" I asked.

"That's appl' jelly made from the early red appl's."

Sold. It would be a sweet touch added to the assorted gifts already gathered for my mother-in-law, Helen. After church the next day Patrick's parents, Jack and Helen, were coming for dinner. It would be a special afternoon with hamburgers on the grill, a marinated fresh vegetable salad, watermelon, caramel cake, family fellowship and the making of precious memories: a meaningful combination if there ever was one. The Curb Market, yet again, would be making a contribution to the joy of living.

It wasn't too long after this conversation in May, 2008, that Joyce came to Elaine Staton, the Curb Market manager, and said simply, "I figure hit's time to b' done." So Joyce Pace is no longer a fixture at the Market. It's a personal loss for all of us. Oh, how we'll miss you, Joyce, and this time you won't be back.

As mentioned before, later that summer the Curb Market held a retirement party to honor three of its dearest members, each one a Market vendor and stock holder for over 50 years: Joyce Pace, Hoyte Jones, and French "Pop" Rogers. What a wonderful opportunity to thank them for their faithful service and to render a final "good-bye."

Chapter Fourteen
Angels, Bonnets, Caramel Cake, and Dolls, Etc.
Marilyn Pryor Horne
Baker and Seamstress Supreme

Marilyn Horne
(Photo by Ann Wirtz)

The gentleman pointed to the Caramel Cake and pulled out his wallet. "Excuse me, Sir; do you like her Caramel Cake?" I asked with a smile, knowing my own thoughts on the subject.

"Oh, my goodness, I'm addicted to her Caramel Cake! When the grandchildren come, they don't ask for their grandmother's cake, they want Marilyn's!"

"Do you live in the area?"

"I drive up from Tryon (North Carolina). I used to live in Greenwood, South Carolina, but we retired in Tryon several years ago."

"May I ask your name?"

"Peter Hawes."

"Well then, Peter, how did you first learn about her cakes?"

"We were at a dinner party in Hendersonville, over on Kanuga Road. I asked if anyone knew someone who could make Caramel Cake. Immediately, every hand around the table went up, and in unison they all said, 'Marilyn Horne!' My grandmother used to make this kind of cake," he confided.

I was at the Curb Market several months later when I chatted briefly with Holly Robinson, who had driven up from Green River to purchase a Caramel Cake for her dad's birthday. She echoed the same common refrain, "Marilyn's Caramel Cake is legendary."

I remember my own introduction to Marilyn Horne's number one seller. I was studying the desserts at an after-church dinner one Sunday. Slices of multi-layer yellow cake with caramel icing between each layer and crowning the top made it an easy choice. One bite and I had to determine where this amazing dessert came from. After another surreptitious slice, I started asking. It took me several days, but at Wednesday night choir rehearsal I found out. Carolyn Vaughn, who was a librarian for 25 years at the Henderson County Public Library and is now retired, laughed when I asked about the cake and told me she bought it from Marilyn at the Curb Market.

The following Saturday morning I was there to purchase my own Caramel Cake, and I've touted this delectable dessert ever since. It is simply a delicious, satisfying cake, an unparalleled sweet, as many of us see it.

The choice can be difficult, however, when standing in front of Marilyn's counter laden with her other delectable looking cakes: chocolate, coconut, pound and Blackberry Wine Cake. Perhaps I'll try them someday, since I'm confident that along with her Caramel Cake, they'd be just as exquisite with their own taste sensation.

For immediate and easy sweet-tooth satisfaction, her peanut butter cookies, packaged five for a dollar, are a quick pick-up and purchase as one walks past her booth. As we talked one day about her Curb Market experience, several stopped and soon her basket of cookies was almost empty.

I contemplated asking for her Caramel Cake recipe but knew better and stated instead, "Marilyn, I know you'd never share your Caramel Cake recipe."

"No," she responded wisely, "but I will share my cookie recipe. It's an easy one, unusual because there are no eggs in the mix. Actually, my grandson, Wesley Alan, and my husband like to eat the dough before it's baked!"

And with that, she was kind enough to promptly share the following:

Peanut Butter Cookies

1 Box of Jiffy Pie Crust Mix
1 Cup brown sugar
½ Cup creamy peanut butter
3 Tablespoons water

Mix well and form into small balls.
Place on greased cookie sheet.
Use a fork to make the traditional tine-crossed markings.
Bake at 350 degrees for approximately 10 minutes.

Not surprisingly, this easy and delicious recipe came from a fund-raising cookbook, the kind known for its tried and true family recipes. The Curb Market itself has published two such cookbooks over the years, *Curb Market Vittles* in 1977, and *Curb Market Vittles Volume II* in 2003.

When Marilyn got married in 1979, her mother gave her a copy of volume one. "I wore that first cookbook out," Marilyn said. "It's filled with great recipes. One of my favorites is 'Boyfriend Cookies,' which is an oatmeal cookie made with dry-roasted peanuts and chocolate chips. I sell them here, and I'm always asked where the name came from, but I don't know." Perhaps the ingredients themselves contribute to the name, a combination sure to please anyone's beau. The cookbooks are available at the Curb Market today, with the recipes from the ol' timers making each book a keepsake as well as a resource for good down-home eating.

Marilyn continued her story. "My mother never made a caramel cake that I can remember," she observed. "She made coconut cakes, using a real coconut. A coconut has three 'eyes,' but only one is soft, and she'd use an ice pick to poke a hole and drain the milk for us to drink. She'd then take a hammer and bust it open, and as kids we would chip out the coconut she'd use for her cake."

Does anyone do that today? Bags of coconut from the grocery store are so, well, convenient, but aren't we grateful that once upon a time there were "old ways" to accomplish a task?

Marilyn's father, Robert Lee "Bob" Pryor, was born and raised in the Hooper's Creek area; her mother, Goldie Ruff Pryor, grew up in Dana. They married and farmed full-time in Fruitland, where they raised beef cattle and vegetables for Thomas Produce. "Mother was in her early 30s when they married in 1952; my dad was in his 50s," Marilyn said. "I came along several years later, and my brother, Robert Lee Jr., two years after I was born. I was a little bitty girl when Mother started at the Curb Market, and I can't remember her not being here. She sold flowers and made shuck dolls, sun bonnets which I still sell, aprons and a variety of things. As I got older, she would bring some of the sewing and crafts I started making and sell them for me, since I wasn't at the Curb much back then."

Marilyn explained, "I was a daddy's girl growing up, and I was always in the fields with him. I wanted to be outside. I've been told that when I was a tiny thing, around two years old, I fell asleep in my dad's truck on the way to the field. He dropped me off at my aunt's house, which was on the way. When I woke up and he wasn't there, I wasn't too happy about that. Apparently, I never went to sleep in his truck again! I know I never wanted to miss riding the tractor with Daddy as he plowed and planted the fields. Other times, my brother and I would roam and investigate, play in the water ways, find snakes and bees' nests. I have always loved being outdoors!"

As the conversation flowed along, Marilyn also shared memories common to many, "I remember my dad building onto the house we lived in. When I was young, the house only had one bedroom and a small living room, no bathroom, only an outhouse. My dad also taught my mom how to drive, so she could drive herself to the Market. He died in June, 1981, not long before his first grandson was born. I started full-time at the Curb in 1989, and my mother died several years later in 1993. I inherited her booth. My brother has a table next to mine which I use, and I acquired another table, so I have three booths together.

Marilyn is famous at the Market for her cakes and creative sewing, but initially she also brought farm-fresh eggs and beef. After she married Alan Horne, they began farming on land received from her parents, raising their own beef cattle from bottle-fed calves. Their children were born in 1981, '83, and '85: Gary, Daryl, and their daughter Tracy. I must add that rarely have I seen a mother and daughter look so much alike, both beautiful inside and out. Tracy is a former Miss Junior Hendersonville who happens to bake great chocolate-dipped macaroons to sell at her mother's table. Take it from one who knows!

Rural living and a Curb Market heritage define Marilyn Pryor Horne. "I used to work fulltime as a drafting engineer, but when our third child came along and the paycheck went for childcare, my husband and I decided I would stay home and do contract sewing. When the kids were in middle school, we decided as a family to devote our energies to fulltime farming. Alan was able to leave his job on the night shift at Wilsonart in Fletcher, and all of us together worked to raise our own food. We had a dairy cow and the beef cattle, chickens, a garden, and fruit trees; we were a self-sustaining farm. That was a wonderful time for our family. The kids learned how to work hard, something the teachers always commented on in school."

Marilyn added, "For all these years, the Curb Market has always provided extra income for us. Along with the cakes I bake in my convection oven, fresh every Market day, I love to sew, something that's always come naturally to me. I remember making my own clothes in high school, although I never took a Home Economics class. If I wanted something, I made it myself. I now have an industrial sewing machine, but in order to enjoy sewing, I have to make what appeals to me. I love to go to garage sales and thrift stores looking for unusual material, lace, quilts, anything old and used. I give new life to what I find."

The scope of Marilyn's talent and originality is plain to see when looking over the variety in her Curb Market booth. A darling Raggedy Ann Doll caught my attention a while back, and with her navy-blue checked dress adorned with a pale, tea-colored muslin apron and lace collar, both trimmed with buttons, and the dimples on her sweet face represented by tiny hearts: I couldn't resist. Even though I already had a Raggedy Ann which my mother made for me in 1966, one of my most treasured possessions, I decided this more modern version would make a delightful sister, a young Raggedy Annie. And she does.

In summing up her life, Marilyn explained, "Everyday I pray to the Lord, thanking Him for all my blessings. I grew up and was baptized at Fruitland Baptist Church, where our kids were raised and where we still go. It's been a wonderful place for us. I learned something about faith several years ago when it was discovered I have an unusual blood condition. I do believe the Lord put Dr. Radford in my life to help figure out what was going on and to calm me down."

(A side note: There are numerous people who would agree with Marilyn. Dr. James E. Radford Jr., local oncologist and hematologist, has seen many an individual and family through a difficult medical diagnosis. Extraordinary care, compassion, and expertise are the hallmarks of this unique doctor. I understood exactly what Marilyn was saying; Dr. Radford was my late first husband's doctor and is mine.)

Marilyn was eager to describe her experience. "This discovery began late one night when I was icing cakes in the kitchen and got very dizzy. I had been coping with tiredness and panic attacks and feeling miserable because I didn't understand what was going on. I burst into tears and started praying. I told the Lord I wanted peace. I didn't care if I was healed or not, I just wanted His peace. The next morning I felt like a new person!" Marilyn said in amazement. "I tried to continue worrying, but I couldn't do it! The Lord truly kept me in His perfect peace as He then led me to Dr. Radford and to an understanding and control of my condition."

Family, friends and customers are very grateful for this lovely woman. Marilyn's bountiful Appalachian Mountain industry and faith, so representative of the early pioneers of Western North Carolina, are on display at the Curb Market, enriching us all.

Chapter Fifteen
Recipes for Life and Homemade Bread
Ruby Jones King
A Regular for Over 55 Years

Ruby King
(Photo by Ann Wirtz)

The first thing I ever bought from Ruby King was a loaf of whole wheat bread. I ate a slice with butter and strawberry jam, then turned around and ate another! Ruby spends her Fridays making batches of both white and whole wheat bread to be sold at the Curb Market every Saturday.

The loaves are arranged on her counter, her homemade jellies nearby. "I grow my own blackberries to use in the jelly," Ruby shared one day as I observed the jars glistening with a rich intensity impossible to overlook under the counter lights.

She also makes orange marmalade and apple honey, and the dilemma is on for any customer trying to decide which one to purchase. Perhaps all three because, really, they're all delicious and each lends itself to a certain taste combination. Orange marmalade and a toasted English muffin are made for each other. Apple honey would be comforting on a hot, southern biscuit. And blackberry jam is, well, perfect on everything.

"Ruby, your whole wheat bread is so delicious would you consider sharing your recipe?" I ventured one Saturday morning. "If you want to keep it a secret, I certainly understand, but if you'd like to share it, I'd love to include it in this book."

"Well, I don't know why not," she replied kindly. And with her gracious consent, Ruby's recipes are found at the conclusion of this chapter: Ruby's Wonderful Bread and Ruby's Famous Dinner Rolls, which she also sells at the Curb Market.

Of course, this is not all Ruby makes. Her counter is lined with jars labeled Cucumber Relish, Chow-Chow, as well as an assortment of Watermelon, Mustard, and Green Tomato Pickles. She has large quart jars of homemade Kraut, and how delicious that would be with a number of meats.

As we chatted about her delectable offerings, I studied the corn husk dolls she's made, little maidens ready to take their country charm to a good home. During our conversation, Ruby perched on a stool behind the counter, her hands busily fashioning a flower out of a corn husk. Her fingers would deftly curve and tuck until a beautiful lily was ready to sell. She set it in a vase with others of a soft orange or lemon hue, and I chose one of each color. They've become a subtle focus in an arrangement I've fashioned to grace a beautiful, white china pitcher adorned with autumn leaves, a gift purchased in Charleston and given to us by my husband's cousin and wife, our best friends, Kenneth and Angie Rhodes. Ah, just right.

"I used to do a lot of flower arranging," Ruby confided. "For years, I had a wholesale dried flower business with many salesmen. I picked flowers and dried them, wrapped them in green paper, and they were sold as 'Ruby's Bouquets.'

"I bought a piece of property in 1982 behind Bloomfield's Dish Barn (now Bloomfield's of Flat Rock) over on I-26. It included a 100 year old house, in which I started a shop called Country Village Crafts. I sold flowers and nice gifts. After the first six years, I built a beautiful log cabin for the business, which I ran for almost 20 years. I sold the property in 2006. I've always had good employees who could manage the store while I came here to sell. You see, I've been selling at the Curb Market since 1953. I didn't inherit my table; I'm the only one from my family who's ever worked here."

I wanted to know, of course, what brought her to the Curb.

Her earnest reply: she wanted to be a stay-at-home mom. Ruby explained, "When our oldest son, Joe Jr., went to first grade, that's when I started. I needed to supplement our income and thought this would work. I sold whenever I could get a booth until I was assigned a permanent place and became a stockholder."

It was apparent from the start of our conversation that Ruby has always worked hard. I was curious how she'd describe her motivation. Her quick response reflects her life from the 1930s and '40s.

"Poverty," Ruby stated emphatically. "Growing up poor, I learned to work early in life. I was born in Henderson County in 1926, the youngest of four children. My mother died when I was five years old. My dad farmed in the Upward community, and he lost everything in the Great Depression. He remarried when I was 13.

"I've always worked on the farm and helped take care of the house and the family. When I was 17, I took my first job away from the farm at Chipman Lacrosse, which was a hosiery mill in East Flat Rock. I was paid 12 ½ cents an hour. From there, I went to Grey's Hosiery Mill in Hendersonville. I didn't particularly like either job because I always wanted to be outside in the sunshine! Back then, the mill let me work part of the year, so I was able to be at home when I was needed and then go back."

Her story continued, "I married Joseph Basil King when I was 19. We had two sons, Joe Jr. and Douglas, and both still live in Henderson County. I have four grandchildren and three great-grandchildren. I'm not the kind of person who brags a lot, but I'm so proud of all of them! In 1983, my husband died from cancer. Through everything, though, I've stayed with the Curb Market."

When I asked Ruby how she views the whole of her life, tears came to her eyes as she declared, "The Lord has blessed me. I have my health and the ability to do and learn new things every day. I was 82 on March 5 (2008), and I'm grateful for the life I've had."

Recipes for the staff of life and a recipe for life itself: Ruby shared more with me than she realized. She unknowingly offered the true and tested ingredients for personal satisfaction, fulfillment and success. Ruby's life has been a testimony to hard work, the power of a can-do spirit, and a willingness to try creative ventures. More important than even these attributes, however, has been her devotion to faith, family and a love for others. Her comprehensive approach to life is a recipe we'd do well to follow. Thank you, Ruby!

Ruby's Wonderful Bread

Sour Dough Starter:
¾ Cup sugar
3 Tablespoons instant potatoes
1 Cup warm water

To Make Bread:
½ Cup sugar
1 Cup starter
½ Cup corn oil

To Feed Starter:
¾ Cup sugar
3 Tablespoons instant potatoes
1 Cup warm water

1 Teaspoon salt
1 ½ Cups warm water
6-8 Cups Bread Flour
    For Whole Wheat Bread:
    3 ½ cups Whole Wheat Flour plus
    2 ½ to 4 ½ cups White Flour

To Prepare Starter:
Mix ingredients well and let stand out of refrigerator all day: 8-10 hours.
Remove 1 Cup mixture and return the rest to the refrigerator – keep covered.
To keep Starter active, you must feed it every 3-5 days.
If you aren't making bread after each feeding, remove 1 Cup Starter and give the rest to a friend, or throw away.

To Make Bread:
Mix all ingredients into a stiff dough and put into a large bowl (greased).
Cover lightly with plastic wrap.
Leave over night, or 8-10 hours.
Punch down with fist and let rest 10 minutes.
Divide into 3 equal parts and knead each part on floured surface.
Place in greased loaf pans.
Brush with oil and let rise 10-12 hours (depending on temperature).
Bake at 350 degrees for 30 minutes.
Cool on rack.

Ruby's Famous Dinner Rolls

1 Teaspoon Sugar
¼ Cup warm water
1 Package dry yeast
1 Cup milk
1 Egg
1 Teaspoon salt (scant)
¼ Cup sugar
¼ Cup shortening – melted
3-3 ½ Cups bread flour

Add the 1 Tsp. sugar to the warm water.
Sprinkle the yeast over the water and stir.
Set aside for 3-5 minutes.
In a large bowl, combine the milk, egg, salt, ¼ Cup sugar, melted shortening. Mix well.
Add the "proofed" yeast and stir.
Gradually begin adding the flour until you have added as much as you can stir with a spoon.
Place dough on a lightly floured surface and knead for 5-8 minutes or until dough is smooth.
Shape into a ball and place in greased bowl.
Cover and let rise until doubled (about an hour).
Punch down, remove from bowl and allow to rest, covered, for about 10 minutes.
Shape as desired, cover, and allow rolls to rise for another 30 minutes.
Bake at 400 degrees for 12-15 minutes.

Yield: 24-30 Dinner Rolls

Chapter Sixteen

A Way of Life
Mary Staton Jones
One Family's Heritage

Mary Jones
(Photo by Ann Wirtz)

"It's a way of life, really," Mary Staton Jones said about the Curb Market one Tuesday afternoon in early June. "I wouldn't know what to do if I didn't come." Mary sat behind her booth located by the northwest side entrance, jars of pussy willows, plants, and tansy in pots almost hiding her from sight. I had talked with her briefly before, her sweet smile a welcoming encouragement to stop and visit.

"My mother and dad, Robert and Lucille Henderson Staton, got their Curb Market stock in 1933, and I was born in 1934. I was raised on a farm out 64 East in the Uno section, about a mile from where North Henderson High School is today. I've lived in Fruitland for many years, since I married my husband Bill Jones. He was from Transylvania County. He was working in town and staying with my uncle, who introduced us. I was 23 when we got married, and we had one son, Thomas, who inherited my sister Arlene's Curb Market stock when she died in 2002."

Arlene and Mary are two of Robert and Lucille's six children. Their grandmother was Pearl Barnwell Henderson, who started at the Curb Market on King Street in the early 1930s. All Pearl's daughters either started with her or soon joined the Market: Louise Edmundson, Lucille Staton, Irene Corn, and Mallee Corn.

According to the 1999 "book of memories," Pearl sold the variety of farm produce and flowers the Market is famous for. She specialized in a well-known flower, the Black-Eyed Susan, and one can imagine there are many still growing in the county that originated on her farm. She was known for wearing a black hat, sitting on a big stool, and treating herself to the homemade sugar cookies she'd buy from Mrs. Jep Williams.

Mary talked about Pearl's daughters, and the "book of memories" added a few tidbits of information that reflect an era long past. "Irene and Mallee sold together on the same table," Mary explained. "They were married to twin brothers from the Corn family. Louise always worked with her mother."

Irene started at the Market in the late 1930s, and Mallee joined her several years later. Together, they were known for their farm products, flowers, and the cured hams Irene sold next to the fresh, dressed chickens Mallee prepared for her regular customers. Two were so faithful, their names made it into the "book of memories:" Mrs. Duff and Mrs. Byrd. This often happens, a comfortable relationship, even friendship, between vendors and repeat customers. Along with this, the memoir reveals a bit of delightful early mountain vocabulary, *"After a trip or two,* (Irene) *always said 'paper bag' instead of 'poke.'"*

Irene was at the Curb until 1950, when she unfortunately died from Lupus Disease at the young age of 40. Irene's husband, Elbert, kept things going for a while longer until he finally gave up the table when her sister Mallee stopped coming.

From the beginning Mary's mother, Lucille, had her own booth at the Curb Market. Her offerings included the traditional wide range of goods, and then some: vegetables, apples, plums, cherries, different kinds of berries, buttermilk, butter and eggs, fresh pork, cured ham and side meat, dressed chickens, and rabbits during the hunting season. In the "book of memories" an intriguing, even startling sentence is added to explain that *"everyone had to leave a hind foot on each rabbit to prove it was a rabbit and not a cat."*

FitzSimons provides an answer to this curious statement in Volume III of *From The Banks of The Oklawaha*, Chapter 59. *"When a boy caught a wild rabbit, skinned and dressed it for sale, the fur was always left on one of the hind feet. This was required so that the purchaser could know the animal being sold was actually a rabbit. At the beginning of one winter a rumor spread through town that some boys were killing and skinning cats for rabbits. The market for rabbits was completely wiped out until some wise person came up with the idea of leaving the fur on one hind foot for identification. The rabbit market immediately revived."* (1)

The Curb was an outlet for the whole family. Mary's older sister, Arlene Staton, was nine years old when their mother began here. Eventually, Arlene took over Lucille's table and continued selling the items they were known for, adding jellies, pickles and chutney. Mary's brother and his wife, Herbert and Bonnie Mullinax Staton, joined the Curb in 1963, providing apples, vegetables, and friendship for all who stopped by.

After 45 years, Bonnie is still at the Curb Market, where customers stop by for her cherries, a bumper crop the spring of 2008. "I like to come here," she said as we sat together behind her table on a busy Saturday morning after cherry season had passed. This day she was selling fresh dill and cucumbers from her garden and assorted pots containing the succulent plant known as Hen and Chicks. "It's a fun place to be. I've known a lot of people over the years, and I miss the ones who are gone. My husband, Herbert, died six years ago from cancer. I was married to the best guy in town, and we were together at the Market all these years. Don't know how much longer I will continue though. It's getting harder to plant the seeds, and the groundhogs eat my greasy beans," she said with a resigned smile. "Our four children aren't interested in taking this table because they're busy with other things. Herbert's mother, Lucille, got us involved; she loved it here, and so have I."

Mary's Curb Market story encompassed not only family members and friends, but fortunately some about herself as well. "I've been coming to the Curb since I was a little girl," she reminisced softly. "I helped my mother, and then my son grew up here, too, helping me. He took over my sister's booth, and today he and his wife, Toni, sell vegetables on the table next to mine. He's a fourth generation seller. I can't ever remember not being here. My sister and I sold on the lot outside the old Farmer's Market on Greenville Highway during the construction of this building. After I got married, I continued here while my husband worked at G.E."

With her sister's table on one side, Mary had a good friend on the other side, Bertha Lanning Pryor, who was known for her woven rugs and her unusual potholders. The "book of memories" reveals Bertha started at the Curb with her mother, Eliza Nix Lanning, when the Market was still on King Street. They embroidered bedspreads and pillow covers, and made handbags and pocketbooks. This rounded out the usual farm items they sold to their regular customers. Eliza died in 1959, and Bertha continued for another twenty years until her death from cancer in January, 1980.

Her words laced with sadness, Mary said quietly, "Lots of wonderful people have come and gone. Some have died or they've moved on, but when they're no longer with us, it can be lonely."

Mary was echoing a familiar sentiment. The day comes when someone who's been at the Market a long time is no longer here. New vendors come, as they should, but first-hand memories and yearnings still remain for the ol' timers. They're simply irreplaceable. Russ Lyda eventually got Bertha's table, where he sells vegetables, flowers and apples from his orchard, and he and Mary have become good friends.

As she has done through the years, Mary continues to sell her pickles, jams, and the lovely plants and flowers that brighten her booth. I can especially attest to her fresh strawberry jam, so delicious it evokes thoughts of sunshine, rain and the good earth! It definitely adds the perfect touch to cream cheese spread on toast. Mary has worked alone at the Curb for most of her life, explaining, "My husband only came with me in his last years, after he retired from G.E. He died from Parkinson's disease in 2004."

Mary's lifetime faithfulness to the Curb Market is best understood through her own words, spoken on behalf of so many here, "It's a way of life." A glimpse of this life permeates each story and remembrance about the Curb, and we're grateful for the telling.

Chapter Seventeen
Lining up for Iris, Peaches, Apples and Plants
Russell Lyda
Spring, Summer, Fall and Winter

Russ Lyda
(Photo by Ann Wirtz)

"I've been selling here since 1977, when I got my own table," Russ Lyda shared one busy Saturday morning. The Curb Market was humming with shoppers, and plants and flowers seemed to be among the hot items, not surprising for mid-June. Russ' assistant for the 2008 summer season was Lindsay Corn, an upcoming senior at North Henderson High School. Both were helping customers as they lined up in front of Russ' table to purchase plantings of purple Japanese iris and pink and blue hydrangea.

During the occasional lull, Russ would arrange vases of blue larkspur and orange butterfly weed, enhanced with blades of Johnson grass and Queen

Anne's lace, a combination of color and delicacy so appealing the bouquets sold about as quickly as Russ could combine them. Later in the season, he put together another beautiful, eye-catching arrangement using Black-Eyed Susan, yarrow, butterfly weed, Queen Anne's lace, and purple allium, simply stunning. The end of February, he brings in pussy willows and the dramatic curly willow which announce spring is less than a month away; good news after a weary winter.

Russ has much to share about the Curb Market of yesterday and today. "The country people used to make out fairly well here, even during the Depression," he said thoughtfully. "They would've been in dire straits otherwise, without the Market. It was not unusual for my Grandpa Lyda to make a dead fall trap and sell quail and rabbits. He'd tack 'em up and down the posts along with dressed chickens," he said, pointing to the posts on both sides of his booth. All four of his grandparents sold at the Curb, John and Pearl Brown Lyda, and Tom and Milda Guice Orr. His mother, Christine Orr Lyda, received her parent's table when they retired.

According to the "book of memories," the Lydas began selling at the Curb Market around 1930, and the Orrs began in 1937. John and Pearl Lyda had a table at the Curb for 32 years, where they sold a fine selection of fruit: apples, cherries, quinces, gooseberries and black raspberries. A number of pies and cobblers have undoubtedly been made through the years with fruit from the Lyda farm! Vegetables, flowers, and Pearl's pound cakes rounded out their offerings. When he wasn't working their table, John also attended to the Curb parking lot.

The Orrs were very involved, too, with Milda serving on the Board of Control for several years. The Board members always looked forward to an evening at the Orr home, where fresh coffee accompanied one of Milda's famous cakes, baked and served for the Board meeting. She sold a variety of pound and layer cakes, according to the "book of memories," including applesauce, brownstone, caramel, chocolate, coconut, devils food, oatmeal, and pineapple cake.

I had never heard of a "brownstone" cake before but found an answer in *The Encyclopedia of American Food and Drink* by John Mariani. (1) The cake was identified as a *"brownstone front cake,"* a rich chocolate cake with a vanilla or caramel icing. Recipes for the cake date back to at least 1903, but the origin of the cake is unknown. The name is thought to refer to the reddish-brown facade of a brownstone building.

Along with Milda's baked goods, the Orrs were also known for their vegetables and meats. Their farm was located next to Frank L. FitzSimons, and the two families grew produce together which the Orrs would sell at the Curb.

Their combined efforts make another remarkable list: beans, beets, bell peppers, broccoli, cabbage, cauliflower, corn, okra, onions, potatoes and tomatoes. Accompanying the produce were cured hams, dressed fryers, buttermilk and butter. The Orr and Lyda families made their livings here, as most of the vendors did in the early years, the economic benefit from the Curb Market simply incalculable.

The Orrs retired in 1983 after 46 wonderful years, their smiles in their "book of memories" photo a testimony to their Curb experience. They passed their table to their daughter, Christine, who used her talents and interests to showcase homemade items including bonnets, quilted jackets, and vests. Her variety reflects the broader focus of the Market in these latter years.

"Over time," Russ explained, "the Curb Market has become more of a weekend market, with 85% of our business now on Saturdays. I think with plant and local produce stands on every corner, or so it seems, and even in the grocery stores, our Market is not the central location for food that it once was. But at the Curb there's an important connection, because here the customer buys directly from the people who grow the food. It's interesting, the general ignorance out there about farming. Many, if not most of us are only a couple generations away from the farm as it was in the 1930s, '40s, and '50s. Yet people today, especially kids, don't have a clue where food comes from, except from the store."

Russ knows his subject. Growing up with a farm background, he graduated from Edneyville High School and then received a degree in horticulture from North Carolina State University. This serves him well as he cultivates and sells his plants, flowers and fruits, including apples, berries, cherries, peaches and plums.

"The Curb Market is a good place for a vendor, because you can take something that might be considered worthless and turn it into money," Russ exclaimed. "I can take lambsquarter and Johnson grass, which you don't want in your garden or field, and make a beautiful arrangement with them.

"Matter of fact our son Nathan, who teaches social studies and coaches basketball at Flat Rock Middle School, has made the best sale ever here," as Russ tells it. "He sold skipping stones for 25 cents apiece. A guy wanted some for his pond. I think that's pretty amazing!"

After a break to interact with his customers and sell some of his breathtaking bouquets, Russ continued, "There are a lot of interesting characters here, both selling and buying, and that's what makes this a unique place to be. People are trustworthy, for the most part. I've only had two checks returned since I started. My family is involved, with lots of moral support from my wife Teresa (Drake Lyda), who is a Distance Learner Facilitator and Teacher Assistant at North Henderson High School. She'll sometimes have crafts to sell. Nathan is pretty regular during the summer months, and his wife Amanda joins him. Our other son, Todd, is currently finishing his doctorate in genetics at Clemson University. Both boys have grown up attending the Curb."

Teresa shared a mother's perspective. "I remember when Nathan and Todd were younger they used to play under the table with their Hot Wheels and Lego toys while we sold. They both have learned valuable lessons on how to deal with people, and both are still spoiled by all the attention they got from our neighbors! It was a wonderful place for them to grow up."

Russ, who has served on the Board of Directors, made a telling observation about the people of the Curb and their connection to each other. "I'm probably related to most of the people here, one way or another." And that interconnection is a big part of the Curb Market story, soon approaching a century of commerce.

The Russell Lyda family is continuing the tradition that began in 1930 with John and Pearl, and the story is not finished yet. When the 100th Anniversary of the Curb Market occurs in 2024, the story-line will be families who are still here with roots deep in the soil of the Market's history. While the future is unknown, of course, the Curb and its members will continue moving forward into the 21st century, providing a link to the past and opportunity for the future.

Chapter Eighteen
Oh, Those Deviled Eggs
Earl and Mary Frances "Fran" Hudson Griffin
Keeping Tradition Alive

Fran and Earl Griffin
(Photo by Ann Wirtz)

It was Christmas time at the Curb Market, 2008, and vendors were doing their part to promote the holiday with gift ideas, decorations, and festive food for the gatherings and parties sure to take place. I was holding a book signing, my short story in *A Chicken Soup for the Soul Christmas*, 2007, my contribution to the season. I was located near the southeast corner of the Market, where Earl and Fran Hudson Griffin have long held the table originally belonging to Earl's aunt and uncle, Willis and Beatrice "Bea" Griffin Allen. There was a lot of early activity at their booth, obviously regulars who knew exactly what multiple items they wanted to purchase. As they walked away laden with bags and trays of food, I decided I'd better not wait too long to introduce myself to Earl and Fran and to the delectable looking variety that covered their counter.

Their amazing assortment ranged from the sweet to the healthy:
Chocolate Fudge
Pumpkin Pie Fudge ~ deliciously sweet and a touch healthy,
made with pumpkin harvested from their own patch
Brownies
Apple Pie ~ with apples from a brother's orchard
Black Walnut Pound Cake ~ with walnuts from their own tree
Lemon Pound Cake
Orange Slice Cake ~ made with orange slice candy, coconut and pecans
Muffins ~ blueberry, peach and honey bran
Apple Squares ~ always made with Golden Delicious from the family farm
Cookies ~ oatmeal raisin and chocolate chip
Lemon Squares
Lemon Cream Cheese Bars
Cream Cheese Coconut Bars
Pickled Okra and Pickled Cayenne Peppers
Pepper Relish
Green Beans
Vegetable Ssoup ~ *absolutely delicious!*
Every bit of this nutritious soup is homegrown and prepared.
Add some browned ground beef, if you're so inclined,
and you've made a meal that satisfies to the very soul.
And then there were the deviled eggs.
Oh my,
even my husband thought they were perhaps the best he'd ever eaten.
The recipe was developed by Aunt Bea (Allen) herself,
years and years ago in the late 1920s.
Now, it's possible I didn't record every single item
Earl and Fran made and sold that day,
but I've come close!

Fran, the cook for all this bounty, stays busy preparing for Market days. "The soup is the most time-consuming to make, but we sell a lot of it. I don't let anything go to waste from the garden. I do my baking and cooking on Monday for Tuesday, on Wednesday for Thursday, and on Friday for Saturday. I've done this for years, preparing the food even though I worked fulltime."

While everything Fran makes is simply delicious, her soup is so legendary, people drive from Florida, Georgia, and all around the state just to buy caseloads of it. Earl shared a remarkable story. "A man and his wife bought a quart jar of the soup and took it back home to Florida. We got a phone call from them saying they ate it all at one meal and wanted more. They asked us to send three cases of soup, but we couldn't do that. Since they're going to Atlanta for the holidays, the plan is to meet them half way there the week before Christmas and sell them 36 quart jars of soup!"

After Bea died, Earl and Fran acquired her booth in 2003. "I worked with Aunt Bea and Uncle Willis when I was young and every Saturday for the six or seven years before I married Fran in 1961," said Earl. "They lived in Fruitland and never had any children, so I was close to them. Larry Anders from Brevard came over and helped Bea for over 20 years. She kind of adopted him. He and his mother still come over and visit us. Bea was in a nursing home for several years before she died, and Fran and I ran the booth during that time.

"Bea worked at the Curb all her life; she loved being here," Earl explained. "She and Willis made a very good living from the Market. Bea was famous for her jellies; she loved making jelly! She'd also make those deviled eggs to sell three days a week, 15 packages containing six eggs each and never take a package home. They sold quite a variety, from nursery plants to the sausage they made from their own hogs."

In the 1999 "book of memories," the first entry is titled "Bea Allen." She writes, *"I have been selling at the Curb Market for 73 years. When I first began selling at the Curb Market I was about 13 years old. I would ride with my uncle and aunt, Ulysses and Brownie Griffin, in their Model T Ford from the Fruitland area. I wanted to make enough money to attend Fruitland Institute where I got my high school diploma in 1930. When I first began selling...I mainly sold wildflowers and berries, such as blueberries, blackberries and strawberries. I also sold milk, butter and eggs that my mother had."*

Bea started at the Curb in 1926 and married Willis in 1930, after she graduated from high school. She continues her story, *"By this time I was making cakes, muffins, potato salad, chicken salad, deviled eggs, jellies and jams to sell at the market. Willis was working in the nursery business so we began bringing different shrubs to sell at the market also. This included azaleas, roses, and many other assorted bushes and flowering trees. During our early marriage, the money we made at the Curb Market was used to build the house that we have lived in throughout our marriage."*

Willis died in November, 1993. Bea kept her booth at the Market, coming mostly on Tuesdays and Saturdays. In her memoir, Bea concludes, *"I feel that continuing at the Curb Market helped with the loneliness that I experienced after losing my dear husband of 63 years. At the market I am able to visit with customers and friends that I have made through the years...I hope that once I am unable to be at the market that (family) will keep the tradition alive."*

As it turned out, Earl and Fran became the guardians of the Griffin Curb Market tradition, especially after Earl retired from Wilsonart. Their tireless devotion to maintaining the variety and superior quality of food established from the beginning represents the essence of the Market today. While the Griffin's two daughters have not indicated a desire to keep the booth once their parents retire from the Curb, Earl and Fran will continue to provide their best as long as they're able.

Reflecting on the Market, Fran shared a familiar refrain, "I love seeing and meeting the people. I've made friends from all over, and there are many who have taken my soup and other foods back to Florida. This became my full-time 'hobby' in 2007, when I retired from my job at Dampp-Chaser. I'm able to do more now, but I've always kept Earl with something to bring."

Earl's Curb highlight echoed his wife's: he loves meeting the people. He added a second reason for their Market faithfulness, one any vendor, ol' timer or new, would agree with, "I enjoy the benefits we reap, when we do." The bounty provided by this dear family is appreciated by legions of regulars and visitors alike. It's a fact: Once you've tried their food, you'll be back for more!

Chapter Nineteen
Venetian Art Glass and Sourdough Bread
Myra, Patrick and Megan Dolan
Food and Beauty for the Soul

Megan and Myra Dolan
(Photo by Ann Wirtz)

Their Curb Market table goes back to Ethel Duncan Case, an aunt from Myra Case Dolan's family who started selling here in the early 1950s. According to the "book of memories," Ethel showcased her creative and culinary abilities each week with everything from baby quilts and placemats to pickled beets and sauerkraut, with fresh and dried flower arrangements rounding out the beauty. Ethel's daughter and son-in-law, Jesse and Julia Case Staton had an adjacent table where they, too, sold a variety of items.

Fast-forward to 2009, and the family talent is manifested through the amazing blown glass pendants, marbles and artistic Venetian Art Glass made by Patrick Dolan. It's also evident in the assorted and delicious sourdough breads made by his family: grandmother, Juanita Taylor Case; mother, Myra Case Dolan; and sister, Megan. During the winter months with Juanita in Florida, Myra and Megan bake the 18 loaves of bread which they bring to the Market for their customers, regular ones who stop by and those visiting the Curb.

The day I had my book signing in December my booth was next to Megan's, and I had the opportunity to enjoy her company, purchase her excellent bread, and learn about the stunning artisan crafted glass jewelry and other items that sparkled beneath the display lights. Some of the glass pendants had an opal tucked inside making a beautiful piece of jewelry that would be a treasure to own.

Megan explained how unusual it is to find such a pendant. "For the past few years, Patrick is one of only a handful of artists on the east coast doing opal encasements," she declared proudly.

These beautiful pieces are sold separately or on silver or gold necklace chains, adding to the variety of jewelry that tempts with unique colors, beads and semi-precious stones. I've always loved garnet, harking back to a gift I received in college from my Aunt Agnes, so Megan's garnet necklace caught my fancy, and I was able to purchase it another day.

The Venetian Art Glass, or Murano Glass, that is Patrick's specialty has a fascinating history, beginning around 982 in Venice, Italy. After 300 years, the Doges of Venice decreed the furnaces for making this glass be moved to the island of Murano, about one mile away. (1) Since a Doge was an elder known for his shrewdness and elected for life by the local aristocracy to be the nominal head of all the governing bodies, this decree was honored. There was a dual purpose for the move: to alleviate the fear of fire from the furnaces and to maintain the secrets behind this exquisite glass, known for its bubbles and ribbons of color. (2) That the Curb Market in Hendersonville, North Carolina, carries artistic glass in the style of this centuries old art form is representative of the unusual talents and variety of items on display here each week of the year.

Since the Curb began in 1924, many of the vendors have come from the Dana area, just south of Hendersonville. This family is no exception. Juanita's parents, Edgar T. and Hattie Ledbetter Taylor, had a farm in Dana where Juanita grew up. Country life is still cherished by this family. For those who love country living, whether from actual experience or from an inherited inclination that fosters a yearning for this way of life, there's nothing better. Like the Dolans, the majority of those who sell at the Market today are still part of the agricultural, rural-life tapestry that was historic Henderson County.

I had the opportunity to speak with Myra one day about their Curb Market experience. She began, "My mother, Juanita, started selling jams and jellies for Linda Justice, whose family still has a booth at the Curb. She soon became addicted to meeting various people, either meeting the locals, family or the traveling types who stopped by. My dad Eugene joined her in selling the jellies because he, too, liked the ability to re-acquaint himself with some old friends and to meet plenty of nice people. They put their name on the list to come sell at the Curb, and being at the right place at the right time, they were given Ethel Case's old table. I started stringing semi-precious beads, some with and some without glass pendants, and my parents began selling my work. Actually, I started stringing beads to quit smoking and fell in love with the creativity!"

Another avenue of work got Myra directly involved in the Market. "I've spent most of my life caring for the elderly in Hendersonville and the surrounding area. My second longest, care-taking experience was working for Ida Freeman, who had a table here and sold loop rugs even before her children were born. She sent most of them to college working at the Curb. She wanted to make sure her children had better opportunities in life than she had. We would go to the Curb three days a week to sell her rugs, and my job was to remember all the things Ida had forgotten," Myra said affectionately.

When Juanita acquired her own booth and began selling home-made bread, Myra and then Megan got involved, and it's been a family business ever since. Their help allowed Juanita to focus her time and attention in another direction. A devoted seamstress, she has a number of sewing machines, including an Elna, and enjoys embroidering hand towels and special request items. Patrick later added his handmade glass, making this a table that satisfies both the physical body and the artistic soul in each of their customers.

Ah yes, customers. Every purchase at the Curb ties in with history past, present and future, which is quite a thought. As people run in to purchase an item in mind or to spend a few minutes browsing, there is generally an innate appreciation for the vendors and all the Curb represents. Certainly, vendors have an appreciation for their customers, some of whom turn out to be famous.

Three Apollo astronauts once stopped at Ethel's booth, an event recorded in a 1973 article written by Susan Carson for the Asheville Citizen-Times. *"Across the aisle, Mrs. Ethel D. Case is also proud of her blue ribbons, 'but I'm just as proud of those,' she comments, pointing to the signatures of astronaut*s (Wally) *Schirra,* (Walt) *Cunningham, and* (Jack) *Swigert on her booth. 'They came in November, and each bought a case of my goodies. I didn't know who they were until they offered to autograph my table.'"*

The day I met Megan, she shared this family story, adding, "I love the Curb Market; you never know who you're going to meet. Sometimes it's slow, sometimes busy, but there's usually someone to talk to. I enjoy hearing people's stories, and I've heard a lot of them, especially from Florida residents. Since I went to the University of Central Florida in Orlando and also worked at Disney World, there's a connection between us. When I was at Disney World, I learned a lot about guest services, basically how to be friendly and interact with people. That carries over here."

Family news, local events, national and international news, there's always a subject for conversation. Stop by and chat with Megan, Myra, or even Juanita in the summertime, and don't be surprised if you walk away with a loaf of bread, a piece of jewelry, or a contemporary version of centuries-old Venetian Art Glass, all sure to please.

Chapter Twenty
Rustic Creativity
Donald and Doris Dill Moore
Birdhouses, Feeders, and Mountain Laurel Beauty

Doris Moore
(Photo by Ann Wirtz)

At Donald and Doris Dill Moore's table their rustic, wooden birdhouses and feeders are an immediate attraction, carefully pieced together with the bark's pattern shown to its greatest advantage. Irresistible, I thought one Saturday morning as I picked out the perfect birdhouse to hang out back to become a residence for one of the charming little Carolina Wrens we see at our feeders. It's now spring, after all, and the clever, clean design of the birdhouse I bought would surely attract this delightful bird with its musical song. I chose a pine tree for its location, away from the busy feeders we have that nourish the birds and squirrels that come throughout the year: Bluebirds, Blue Jays, Cardinals, Carolina Wrens, Chickadees, Doves, Goldfinch, Juncos, Nuthatches,

Titmice, Towhees, and the Woodpeckers: Downy, Red-bellied and Pileated, all common to our area.

Squirrels both white and gray arrive, too, in anticipation of a good meal every day. One of my chores is to head outside each morning to feed the livestock, as I call it, a container in hand with a mixture of sunflower and assorted bird seeds. The squirrels soon position themselves upside-down as they hang from the top of a couple feeders to dine on the contents inside. We don't mind, as we have a feeder that is successfully squirrel-proof, thanks to our local Wild Birds Unlimited store, so no one goes hungry. This sanctuary, entertaining and convenient, provides a delightful interlude from the daily routine. When Patrick comes home for lunch, the variety of birds and the antics of the squirrels, even the chipmunks, captivate our attention and grant us a wonderful respite. I think of the Curb Market in a similar way, as it can uplift when we step into its world of country charm and creativity.

On this particular early spring morning in 2009, I had stopped to talk with Doris about their inventory and involvement in the Curb. She was very knowledgeable about the birdhouses I admired, pointing out the features that appeal to certain birds. "The deep, rectangular boxes are for Bluebirds, but we also turn gourds into houses for them, too. You want to hang these away from a home, as Bluebirds are skittish," she explained. The attractive, round birdhouses on display would be popular with a variety of birds and nice to observe from a window.

Skip forward almost a year to March 6, 2010 and a visit to the Curb Market by the Governor of North Carolina, Beverly (Moore) Eaves Perdue and her husband Bob Eaves. The Market was alive with excitement from Governor Perdue's visit. She came to the community to highlight both the success of Hendersonville's Main Street businesses and the entrepreneurial spirit of the Curb Market. She spoke with many of the Curb vendors, genuinely impressed and intrigued with the talent and ingenuity on display. Her husband even bought a Bluebird house from Doris, their birdhouses irresistible to him, too! His plans: to hang it at the governor's Western North Carolina residence in Asheville.

Going back to the day of our initial conversation, Doris was pleased to discuss the role the Curb Market has played in their lives. She continued, "I feel like I'm home here. My husband, Donald, likes to come occasionally, but he's mostly busy in the woodworking shop we have at our home in Edneyville, where we've lived for 38 years. That's where he makes the birdhouses, feeders and the other items we sell. He often uses slabs of wood he's picked up from the saw mills, and we grow some of the gourds we use for birdhouses. In the summertime, I also bring in vegetables and eggs."

As we talked, I observed a basket on the counter filled with items called "Rustic Whistles," rustic because these handmade whistles were still covered in bark. Before long, two women stopped and each purchased one for a dollar. Another basket contained whistles that had been turned on a lathe and were smooth to the touch. They sold for two dollars each. The whistles are made out of Mountain Laurel, a beautiful flowering plant that is native to the eastern United States.

Wikipedia tells us the Native American Indian made spoons from the wood of the Mountain Laurel, giving it the companion name Spoonwood. This prized plant is considered a shrub in the northern region of the country and a tree in the mountains of the Carolinas. Doris and Donald have an array of wooden products made from Mountain Laurel. Donald turns the wood on a lathe and clever items appear, including toy canons and holders for candles and small items. Oh, the wonder that comes from man's inventiveness and the lovely wood of the treasured Mountain Laurel!

Dewy Dalton Merrell
(Photo courtesy of the Curb Market)

Doris and Donald have been selling these delightful products since 1983. Originally their booth belonged to Doris' Uncle James Joseph "J.J." and Aunt Mamie Lusk Carver. According to the "book of memories," Mamie (or Aunt Mainney) received her table in 1954 and proceeded to sell farm produce, garden flowers, African Violets and the *"old timey bonnets"* she made. She kept the booth going for many years after J.J. died, but when her eyesight began to fail, she gave the table to Doris.

Donald's family has also been at the Curb Market for generations. His grandmother, Dewy Dalton Merrell, started selling at the Curb *"back in the horse and wagon days."* Dewy would load her wagon with the fruits, vegetables and eggs from her Edneyville farm and bring them to town for her regular customers. Dewy had a granddaughter, Phyllis Ruff Rhodes, who is also at the Curb today with her husband, Freddie Rhodes Jr.

Barbara A. Moore, Donald's sister, contributed to the "book of memories," describing the 50 years their mother, Gladys Merrell Moore (Dewy's daughter), sold at the Curb. Barbara wrote, *"She enjoyed the people that had tables in the Curb Market. She enjoyed the people that she sold to. She made many friends...We have lost some mighty fine people that attended the Curb Market, and that is why it is still going on today."* They are not forgotten, those who came before. Their integrity and efforts sustain the Market even now.

Barbara remains a vendor at the Curb, her booth angled across from her brother and sister-in-law. "I've had this table since Mama died in 1994. I sell raspberries, sugar snap peas, and whatever else I have that's in season. I also can tomatoes," she said one Saturday morning, her jars of homegrown tomatoes lined up for sale. Barbara was happy to reminisce about the Market she knew as a child. "The halls were so full back then you could hardly walk down them. Time has changed a lot of things. Personally, I still love to come out and see the different people."

Longevity and heritage have been the defining attributes of the Curb Market. Today's reality poses a challenge, which Doris touched on in our conversation. "I'm glad I inherited my table. It's a lot of work, but I like being here. The older ones are still the back bone of this place. Our son, Emanuel, comes occasionally, but overall there aren't many young ones here. We also have a daughter, Janet, and it'll be up to them to decide if they want to continue this table after us."

As our time together came to a close, Doris concluded, "I enjoy meeting people and seeing customers who've come from different places. We're grateful for the Curb Market. It's a wonderful place to be."

Oh, yes indeed. It's a community treasure.

Chapter Twenty-One
A Family Tradition
Freddie and Phyllis Ruff Rhodes
Storybook Dolls and Hit & Miss Engines

Phyllis Rhodes
(Photo by Ann Wirtz)

"It's a family tradition, being at the Curb Market," said Phyllis Ruff Rhodes. "Both Freddie's family and mine have been here since the beginning. My grandmother was Dewy Dalton Merrell, and she'd bring her produce in a wagon."

The rain was falling gently outside as we spoke together the last Saturday in September, the aisles inside the Curb nonetheless filled with people participating in the 2009 Fall "Ol' Timey Days" celebration. Fortunately, fans and newcomers to the Curb didn't let the weather interfere with their enjoyment of homemade biscuits baked in a wood burning stove and served one of three ways: with ham, sausage, or gravy. This day, music by Pickin "N" Poundin led by Gail Nesbitt got feet tapping under the canopy, set up rain or shine. The band was composed of several guitars, a banjo, mandolin and fiddle, perfect accompaniment for Gail's lovely voice, clear and true as a mountain stream.

After listening for a time to the lively tunes, I headed inside the Curb to absorb the ambience of a Market bustling with activity. It was wonderful to see the turnout for this 85th Anniversary celebration, a day to honor the history of the Curb Market, active since 1924. It was then I happened by the booth belonging to Phyllis Rhodes, home to her storybook and corn shuck dolls, her adorable "dried apple head" granny dolls, sock monkeys and other clever soft toys. She's a busy woman and not often at the Curb, so I was quick to introduce myself when I saw her behind the table. I was eager to tell Phyllis about the visitor at the last "Ol' Timey Christmas" event who had stopped to admire her Little Red Riding Hood Storybook Doll. It had brought back memories of a similar doll purchased here years ago.

As it turned out, Phyllis had some exciting news to share with me! "I just won a Blue Ribbon at the fair for my Little Red Riding Hood doll," she was pleased to say. "The doll also won Judges' Choice and Best of Show." I was thrilled for Phyllis, this recognition clearly a confirmation of her noticeable talent. She had entered her three-in-one doll in the 16th Annual North Carolina Mountain State Fair held earlier in the month at the WNC Ag Center & Fairgrounds in Fletcher.

This particular morning, most of Phyllis' family was on hand for the Ol' Timey festivities; just their son Mark was absent. Daughter Tracy Rhodes Jacobs was in town from Camp Lejeune, N.C., the largest Marine Corps Base on the East Coast. Her Marine husband had recently been deployed to Afghanistan, and she and their two year old son, Alexzander, were home for a visit. Phyllis' husband, officially Troy Frederick Rhodes Jr. but "Freddie" to all, proudly proclaimed his grandson, little Alexzander, could one day continue the family tradition at the Curb Market.

"My granddaddy, Lee Edward Rhodes, and several other farmers came together with Frank FitzSimons and helped start the Curb," Freddie informed me. "He and his wife, Edith Fisher Rhodes, began here and it's gone on down the line. They sold their farm produce, but Edith was known for her fudge, all flavors, especially chocolate and peanut butter. My dad and mother were here, too, Troy Frederick Rhodes Sr. and Julia Owenby Rhodes, so I grew up at the Curb. Our farm was in Edneyville where they had a greenhouse, and Julia would bring her flowers in to sell."

Two brothers of Granddaddy Lee Rhodes were also part of the Market.

Jim and his wife, Lola Freeman Rhodes, were known for her woven rugs. A memoir in the "book of memories" tells about second brother, Harley and Lexine Merrell Rhodes. Written by their daughter, Velda Rhodes Brown, this account offers a telling glimpse into the scope of their Curb inventory. She concludes with a question worth pondering today.

"(My parents) *of Edneyville attended the Curb Market from 1940 to 1958. Poor health made it impossible to attend longer. Being the parents of 10 children, the extra income was very welcome. They gathered & prepared one day and went to the market the next. It kept them busy. They sold vegetables, fruits, eggs, butter, cottage cheese, and frying chickens. They also picked wild blueberries & wineberries. Lexine grew beautiful dahlias and other cut flowers. They owned Baldtop Mountain where they dug wild purple rhododendrons & azaleas and yellow lady slippers. Lexine would sit for hours and crack black walnuts on a big flat rock used for a step into the corncrib and sell them for 75cents a pint. 'Was this really the good old days?'"*

The past is fascinating, at least for some, with the comparisons between yesterday and today a cause for wonderment. Change, so unending, is sometimes positive, sometimes not. The old days were labor intensive, no question; at the same time, simplicity of lifestyle was perhaps their greatest strength. With the world less intrusive and distracting in those *"good old days,"* genuine fulfillment was often realized in ways we tend to overlook in our modern world.

Velda's parents made their way in life working very hard for seemingly little financial reward for their labor, such as 75 cents for a pint of black walnuts. Perhaps a fair price back then? But as the saying goes, "money isn't everything." I dare say cracking walnuts on the corncrib step offered something besides money: fresh air, a break from household chores, the inner settling that comes from the repetition of a simple task, responsible stewardship of the land's bounty, time to think, even time to talk to the good Lord if Lexine had a mind to.

I'm one who does consider that time period *"the good old days,"* at least parts of it. I recognize and appreciate Velda's honest question, however, and from an "ease" standpoint, I wouldn't necessarily want to trade my conveniences away! The past seems good because of the inner qualities developed from simpler living: resourcefulness, integrity, faith and the plain gumption of people to enjoy life, even in the midst of seemingly endless tasks. They had a basic, stick-to-it resolve and character not so common in our throw-away world, and that's admirable. Couldn't we, too, strive for a kindred simplicity and character to enhance the advantages of modern living? I would hope so.

Vision and resourcefulness led to the founding of the Curb Market, and about 150 years before that the founding of our country. Resourcefulness is an indispensable quality for success, one in abundance within the farming community. Freddie and Phyllis own Rhodes Farm, home to the Hit & Miss engines he brings for the public's enjoyment every "Ol' Timey Days" celebration; weather permitting. Each October Freddie displays his engines, too, at the Farm City Day at Hendersonville's Jackson Park. Later in the month he's at the Antique Engine and Tractor Show at the Ag Center Fairgrounds. His Hit & Miss one-cylinder engines seem to reflect the wherewithal of the ol' time farm spirit, since they themselves were an energy resource before electrical power was available.

"These units were used mostly to benefit the farmer," Freddie explained, "to make electricity when we didn't have power out in the country. These single-engines were used a lot of ways, for powering cane and saw mills, water pumps, and for cutting firewood. I've still got my granddaddy's original cane mill where he made molasses using a unit like this."

An article on the history of antique engines was written by Larry Harding and is available on the Web site of our local Apple Country Antique Engine and Tractor Association (ACAE&TA). Freddie belongs to this organization, as does Larry Ball from the Curb. Ball received the 2008 Member of the Year Award from this group. In his article, Harding identifies the Hit & Miss engine as one of two basic antique engine categories. The other category is Throttle Governed, an engine type used today in lawnmowers and tractors.

Harding explains that thousands of Hit & Miss engines were built at the turn of the century and *"were a boon to farmers and industrialists alike. The farmer with the purchase of just one small engine could now run his cream separator, wood saw, butter churn, corn sheller, feed grinder, gristmill and pump water...The heyday of these heavy single cylinder engines was not to last forever, though. In 1935, the Rural Electrification Administration was created to bring electricity to the countryside lessening the need for engines... Nothing today sounds quite like a Hit & Miss popping along at a show. Let's hope these relics of the past will be here for future generations to enjoy."*

Freddie joins a number of individuals in this community dedicated to preserving the history and legacy of American farm life. They provide opportunities for people young and old to experience a taste of country life from past eras. Along with the establishment of ACAE&TA has been the creation of the Mountain Farm & Home Museum located on Brookside Camp Road in Hendersonville. According to its literature, the museum is "dedicated to the preservation of agricultural and domestic equipment, buildings, implements, utensils, methods and literature indigenous to rural life in 19th (and 20th) century Western North Carolina." Supporters of the museum attend "Ol' Timey

Days" at the Curb, bringing antique equipment or vehicles to set up alongside Freddie's Hit & Miss engines.

A.B. Wexler, president of the museum, was at the 2008 Spring Ol' Timey event and explained the museum contains numerous items used on the farm and in the home from the past 100 or more years. Displays at the museum include a grain reaper, circa 1850, as well as a doctor's buggy, and a threshing machine from the early 1900s. Between Freddie's engines and the museum's antique offerings, visitors to "Ol' Timey Days" at the Curb Market can momentarily step back and relish farm history through the ol' time equipment on display.

Fortunately, visitors can experience a bit of history each Market day through the ol' time farm families still sellin' at the Curb.

Chapter Twenty-Two
The Toy Maker of the Curb Market
Velton A. Searcy
Poet and Toy Maker Extraordinaire

Velton A. Searcy, Toy Maker
(Photo courtesy of Sandra Searcy Capps)

Velton A. Searcy was known as both "The Toy Man" and "The Toy Maker of the Curb Market," and the plentitude of unique, ol' timey wooden toys on display at his booth attest to these worthy titles. I stopped by his table in May and sadly learned I was too late to talk with him personally. Velton had died on April 24, 2009, just a month before my visit. Although he had not been at the Curb for a while due to the reoccurrence of cancer, perhaps a conversation could have been arranged. Unfortunately, our one-on-one discussion about his experiences at the Curb Market never happened.

On this particular day, however, his daughter Sandra Searcy Capps and her husband Frankie were both at Velton's booth. Despite their recent loss, they were determined to carry on her family's Curb Market tradition which began when the Market was still on King Street. "This is our first day since Papa died, and it's difficult," Sandra said with tears, "but I grew up under this table, and we're going to try to keep the booth going. Frankie will make the toys. Papa loved this place, and one of his last questions before he died was, 'How're the folks at the Curb Market?' We owe it to him to be here."

Velton was born in Henderson County in 1924, and he was just a few weeks shy of his 85th birthday when he died. Most of his life revolved around the Curb, where he first came with his mother, Geneva Drake Searcy. When Velton was 18, he joined the United States Navy and later wrote in the "book of memories," *"My coming to the market was interrupted by the Second World War."* The Military Funeral Honors which accompanied his burial at Shepherd Memorial Park were a fitting tribute to his service.

Following the war, Velton returned to Hendersonville and *"started back in the old Curb Market"* he loved, joining his mother and sister, Valdarine Searcy Gasperson. He was married by then, and his wife Irene Gasperson Searcy, sister to Valdarine's husband, began making dolls to sell here. She specialized in the three-in-one storybook dolls that became especially popular, creating quite the variety which included: Goldilocks with the Three Bears, Little Red Riding Hood with Grandmother and the Wolf, and Mary and her Little Lamb. Sandra recalled the Snow White doll which had the Seven Dwarfs fashioned as finger puppets and attached to her skirt. When President Jimmy Carter was in office, a friend of the Searcy family worked as a secretary in the White House and gave First Daughter Amy Carter a full set of Irene's dolls.

"My mother was one of three or four doll makers at the Curb Market back then," Sandra explained. "Grandmother Geneva taught her. Some dolls were sent to Knott's Berry Farm in California because someone stopped here and saw them. Tourists would come through the Market and request items be sent all over the country. Mama always had a card tucked in the bodice of her dolls so people could get back in touch with her."

Perhaps the record for the farthest distance any item from the Curb Market has traveled belongs to Velton himself. In 2006, he sent a case of his wooden toy spinners to his grandson, Simon Peter Huntley, who was serving in the military and stationed in Iraq. The wooden spinners were for the Iraqi children. What a delightful picture: A treasured American soldier demonstrating how the spinners work; then handing them out to the curious children on Iraq's city streets. On a one-on-one level, Velton's kindness undoubtedly contributed to some easing of tension in this troubled country.

As decades passed, the poignant changes common to life occurred as well at the Searcy Curb Market booth. Velton noted them without fuss in his "book of memories" account. *"After his retirement, my dad* (Dexter) *started coming* to the market. This continued until my mother and Valdarine quit. Irene and I continued until her death (1986). Since then, I have been coming in alone with my wooden folk toys."

Velton remained faithful to the Curb despite the loss of his wife just weeks before retirement. They had looked forward to many productive years together at the Market, which made her untimely death even harder. Irene had been a dear partner in all they had accomplished, and going on without her was difficult. For Velton, crafting his specialized toys provided a measure of solace in the lonely days. As with other items sold at the Curb, his toys came to represent the heart of the Curb Market itself, perfectly expressed when Sandra spoke wistfully about her father, "Papa made something that was real, something not found in a box store."

She continued, "In the beginning, Papa would use his talent and skills to hand carve each toy, always thinking of the child whose hands would hold it. As he got older, he started using a saw to cut out some of the pieces." Then she added softly, her thoughts again on his relationships here, "Papa loved the people of the Curb Market, as if they were family."

There is no better example of his affection than his friendship with McKenley McCraw, 9 year old son of Joel and Lamonda Gilbert McCraw. The McCraws are situated several tables down from Velton's booth where they sell quality seasonal plants from Linda's Plants, a local certified garden center established by Joel's parents. Across the aisle is the booth belonging to McKenley's grandmother, Lavon Brigman Gilbert. Many a Saturday has found McKenley at the Curb playing with Velton's ol' timey toys, intrigued with their design. As much as he enjoyed them, McKenley appreciated and loved even more the man who made them.

About their relationship McKenley said simply, his words touched with sorrow at the loss of his friend, "Mr. Searcy was kind of like a dad to me. The first time I saw him, I was around two years old, and I jumped from Granny into his arms! He never forgot that. He was just a great man."

Toys are a bridge between the young and the old, and the sweet connection and lasting memories between McKenley and Velton are a testament to this. Truth is: the lasting impact for good on each other comes from the simplest sources ~ friendship, playfulness, compassion, love. There is no accounting the power of these offerings. Velton was responsible for bringing a lot of good to people of all ages, even outside the Curb Market. He was always loading up boxes of toys for the many students Sandra has taught over the years. His generosity was legendary, and the toys he made, sold and gave away were vehicles for the happiness he brought others.

Fortunately, Velton's unique toys still remain, ready for sale, from the

Happy Hopper grasshopper to the duck with the floppy, rubber feet that walk forward as the toy is pushed. Another one of his irresistible, classic toys is the gymnast who hangs from a double-rope bar and performs tricks up and over the bar and back again as the two sides of the wooden apparatus are gently squeezed together. This intriguing toy is similar to one from my own childhood, so I've added it to my small collection of unusual toys. It's fun to play with, so much so I've paused to give my smiling gymnast the opportunity to show off his admirable skills, and admire him I do. Somehow, I know this is the response Velton hoped for. No wonder he loved to make toys!

Among all the creative choices at his booth, Sandra explained that Velton's signature Appalachian toy was the Gee Haw Whimmy Diddle, made of native Rhododendron. To work the toy, you quickly rub a smooth stick across the notches of a second stick. This causes the propeller at the end of the notched stick to spin either to the right, Gee, or to the left, Haw. It takes some experimentation to determine how best to hold the notched stick, for the direction the propeller spins is determined by the position of the fingers and the use of the smooth stick. Subtle changes make it appear the propeller is responding to the voice commands of "Gee" and "Haw." I finally worked out a relatively smooth technique by combining tips from various sources. This toy is a lot of fun and worth a stop at the Curb to pick one up.

Velton's creativity was not limited to the wood he held in his hands. He also found enjoyment in the descriptive use of language, for Velton was a poet. Two of his poems describe life at its satisfying best, one for the country soul and one for the faithful heart:

Before Breakfast

Awake early before the crack of dawn,
Turn off the alarm, stretch and yawn.
Get up and quickly dress yourself,
And take the lantern down from the shelf.
Put on a coat, button it up tight,
Take the milking pail and step into the night.
As you step outside, breathe the fresh air,
Look at the sky, starlit and fair.
It's good to be up before the sun's glow,
Head for the barn, as straight as you can go.
Feed the horse and then the sow,
Turn out the sheep then back to the cow.
Hang the lantern up on a nail,

And sit down and fill the milk pail.
Look in on the kittens and the mother cat,
Rover walks by, give him a friendly pat.
Fill the water trough and pitch some hay,
Feed the chickens and be on your way.
Back to the house, breakfast is near,
It's time to go to work, daylight is here.

Peace

Quiet moments with God alone
Are like steps that lead to the throne,
Freeing my soul from the burdens of the day,
And bearing me up in a heavenly way,
Giving me joy and peace of mind,
That only in the presence of God I find.

Day after day, the story of the Curb Market rolls on, as it's been doing for decades upon decades. Families have come, and families have gone, but leaving is rarely easy. When I stopped by the Curb one Saturday in January, 2010, I found Sandra packing up her father's toys, clearing out his booth.

"We're closing shop," she said firmly, her eyes red from the tears that accompanied her decision. "My dad has been at the Curb since the 1930s, around 1937 I believe. That's more than 70 years, and now it's over. I wanted to make this work; I promised him I'd try. But you have to do what you have to do, and even though we've given this our best shot, it's been really hard with teaching and everything else. Plus, he's so here, and I'm so immersed in this, it's difficult to get beyond the grief. I know he'd want me to go on with my life."

Sandra will be greatly missed, as will her father's toys, but her decision is perfectly understandable. Though her family will no longer be at the Curb, she'd like to see Velton's toys remain and will make copies of her father's patterns for anyone interested in carrying on his popular designs. Hopefully, someone will come forward to become the toy maker for the Curb Market. Velton would want that.

A hug good-bye and an offer of prayer for comfort reminded Sandra of a truism she's heard her entire life. The "family mantra," as she calls it, stems from the faith and hard work required to survive in the mountains of the 1800s. The timeless message, passed from generation to generation, is passed to us this day: "Work is praying with your hands."

Velton's life modeled this truth; one we'd do well to embrace for ourselves.

Chapter Twenty-Three
Curb Connections
The Hyder, Lyda, Gilbert Families
From Live Chickens to Wild Grape Jelly

Verda Hyder
(Photo courtesy of the Curb Market)

Ol' time family lines weave through the pattern of life and commerce that is today's Curb Market. Aunts, uncles, cousins and children abound like they always have, although not as many. One person I was eager to learn more about because of her family's long connection with the Curb was Eunice Hyder Lyda, daughter of Sylvester Spurgeon "S.S." and Verda Rogers Hyder. I stopped at the Market in early December to talk with Eunice about her legendary family.

Eunice and her husband Garland sell fresh fruit and produce along with cut flowers, plants, handcrafts and baby blankets. Her classic Raggedy Ann and Andy Dolls are prominently displayed, ready to cheer a home with their timeless personalities. All this occurs on Verda's original table, located by the Market's southwest entrance.

"Everyone called my mother 'Granny Hyder,'" Eunice began. "She and my dad were original sellers under the umbrellas on Main Street. They sold when the streets were dirt. She'd always wear her hat to Market (which, according to a photograph, was a classic, soft-brimmed hat that would gently curve and peak around her weathered face). They sold live chickens and eggs, garden produce and flowers. Mother also made quilts to sell."

Eunice and Garland Lyda
(Photo by Ann Wirtz)

Eunice continued, "When Daddy was in bed with cancer, he said to me, 'You're the only one who can take Mother to the Market. If you don't do it, her life will end with mine.' After he died in the early 1950s, I continued to bring her here. I became a member and sold beside my mother and have never regretted my decision. She was faithful to the Curb until she passed away at the age of 93."

The morning I visited Eunice and Garland, their daughter Pat Lyda Mintz was selling beautiful Christmas greenery at the booth across from their table. I was looking for fresh greens to hang outside and found the perfect arrangement, complete with a large red bow. As I made my purchase, Pat stated with matter-of-fact pride, "Granny Hyder was little bitty. Everyone liked her. My family is made up of good, hard-workin' people." And that's certainly a big reason for this family's successful Curb legacy.

Since the booth next to Eunice belongs to her niece, Lavon Brigman Gilbert, it was convenient to speak with her, too. Lavon contributed some fascinating memories about her Grandmother Verda Hyder, cherished memories about kin who were "born up on the mountain." Concerning Granny Hyder, Lavon shared, "Verda worked from sunup to sundown every day. She sewed, did oil paintings of beautiful landscapes, canned, made quilts, and grew wildflowers, all to sell. It seems her flowers were the main thing. She had a lot of wildflowers at her place and at her mother's place high up on Green Mountain in the Fruitland area. Her mother was Emma Lyda Rogers, and she was a true mountain woman. To get to her place you had to cross several creeks, and there were no bridges. She smoked a corncob pipe and lived to be 102 years old. It was another world up there."

Since 1924, the ingenuity of a mountain community has been showcased at the Curb Market. Creativity abounds here, born of an environment that emphasizes the value of what's on hand and the ability to make something of it. Besides the opportunity for commerce, the Curb has also been the hub around which member families have revolved. Eunice and Garland's courtship began appropriately at the Curb. Garland had just returned from serving overseas in World War II and had stopped by the Market to see his Aunt Coela Coston, who was the manager at the time. "I needed a ride home," Eunice recalled with a smile. "I had assured my mother I'd find someone who could help me, and before too long Garland Lyda walked through the door! We were married 63 years this past September 24, 2009. Garland sent money home during the war, so he was able to buy a tract of farmland on Fruitland Road going to Bearwallow Mountain. We've lived there ever since. You could say we've brought up our three children with the help of the Curb Market: our daughters Pat and Marilyn, and our son Kevin who's now running the farm. He sells at the Curb during the summer months and is known by his good corn."

Sylvester and Verda had another daughter active at the Curb Market, Edith Hyder Brigman, Lavon's mother. Edith was known for her pound cakes, which Lavon would often help sell. After she stopped coming, Lavon received her table. "My mother was humble, just the nicest person in the world," Lavon exclaimed. "I started on my own around 1984 and have loved being here. I like selling and the fact you can make something and somebody else appreciates it enough to buy it! I make all my own things, but in the fall I especially love to bring in the bittersweet."

Well, that was enough for a ten minute discussion on the uniqueness of this particular plant. We're both hooked on bittersweet. We both look for its signature red-orange brightness hanging amongst the trees as we travel the county roads. For us, and others, bittersweet is simply the essence of autumn, and when this season is a favorite, bittersweet becomes its elegant symbol. "There's just something about it," Lavon said as she offered a description I agreed with, "It's dreamy and restful."

Not everyone agrees with us, of course, and in the early 2000s, the state government in Raleigh sought to outlaw bittersweet as a nuisance. I had recently moved to the area and was thrilled to discover the abundance of bittersweet here, only to learn of such a disappointing and puzzling dictate. Lavon became one of the leaders in a group I remember reading about who rose up to say, "No!" After all, bittersweet provides an important livelihood for many and is sold by a variety of vendors at the Curb itself. Several from the Market joined Lavon in taking a stand against this potentially destructive decision: Ralph King and his daughter, Cindy Hudgins, and Louise Hill.

I understand from Louise that those in Raleigh who didn't know much about bittersweet believed that cutting this plant to sell caused the seeds to spread and perpetuate growth. The reality is that birds are responsible for spreading the seed, and cutting actually keeps the bittersweet in check. This was the issue that needed to be clarified.

Lavon continued, "We wrote a lot of letters and made a lot of phone calls, and finally some men from Raleigh came up to hear our complaints at a meeting at the AG Center. Several of us spoke, explaining the issue and asking them not take this income away from us. Fortunately, we won this battle, and the bittersweet was saved. I think they were surprised at how strongly we felt."

After enjoying the camaraderie over bittersweet, a customer stopped by and I was able to study Lavon's counter laden with jellies, pickles, baked goods, crocheted items, a bittersweet wreath leftover from the fall season...just a wide, heartwarming assortment which brought pleasure in the looking. Since I usually try to buy something from each vendor I interview, I settled on a jar of Lavon's Wild Grape Jelly.

"This has a wonderful grape-y taste," Lavon explained, pleased with my choice. "I have friends and relatives who go grape picking with me. We pick Fox Grapes by the creek and the smaller Possum Grapes up in the mountains. I don't use much water when I make the jelly, so the flavor stays strong." I must say, I discovered this to be the absolutely best grape jelly I've ever had! I stopped later on to buy several more jars to include in the Christmas boxes for my brothers in Texas and Illinois, knowing they'd be tickled with this Appalachian treat.

I couldn't end our conversation without a few thoughts about Lavon's only grandchild, McKenley McCraw, dear friend of the late Curb Toy Maker, Velton Searcy. "McKenley's the joy and light of my life," she said and added with a chuckle, "He thinks I walk on water." According to Lavon, the table that now belongs to McKenley's parents, Joel and Lamonda Gilbert McCraw, originally belonged to Lamonda's grandmother, Mary Dalton Gilbert. Mary's daughter, Grace Gilbert Albritton, had the table for a while before the McCraw's began selling flowers from Linda's Plants.

The Curb Market is a fascinating tapestry of families with an understandable reverence for their heritage. While the vendor connections may appear extensive and a bit confusing at times, well, they probably are. However, that's part of the Curb's appeal: ol' time family lines which are woven throughout the history of Henderson County and are today, through the Curb Market, shining a light on the roots of this community. Be assured, a visit to the Market is a step into the past, but know, too, it's a step forward as both a visit and a purchase keep this local business viable in today's world.

Chapter Twenty-Four
Fried Apple Pies and Ice Cream
Dorothy Clingenpeel Barnwell and son Frank
Crocheting, Embroidery and those Amazing Potato Bakers

Dorothy Barnwell
(Photo by Ann Wirtz)

Buying fried apple pies from Dorothy Clingenpeel Barnwell has become a weekly occurrence for my family. Patrick's parents are now regular customers, as Jack drives down to the Curb Market specifically to buy four or five pies. They're a favorite, a reminder of the time when Helen used to get up way before dawn to fry up 25 pies for Jack to share with his co-workers at DuPont. They were always gone within minutes of his arrival. Their generosity continues, as my parents enjoy sharing some of the pies they purchase from Dorothy, the fortunate recipients primarily Helen's sister Sudie in Gaffney, South Carolina, and Patrick and me.

Several months ago, Helen decided to make up her own batch of fried apple pies, something she hadn't done in years, and she asked me to join her. Fun! Dorothy's pies were the inspiration, and our mother-daughter sharing would provide insight into this Curb staple. Helen had prepared her apples the day before I arrived, cooking up her chosen Red Delicious fresh from the orchard and seasoned with cinnamon. We rolled out biscuit dough, added the filling, and deep-fried one side and then the other until golden brown. They were great, but it took some doing, which made us appreciate all the more the ease of just stopping by Dorothy's booth to purchase this inexpensive treat.

Actually, stopping by Dorothy's booth is an adventure in variety beyond the coveted fried apple and sweet potato pies she's known for. She offers strawberry-rhubarb and plum jellies along with items to brighten the home: crocheted afghans, holiday and special-occasion cloth napkins, aprons and hand towels sporting eye-catching buttons, all appealing to women browsing the Market.

When I was visiting Dorothy one drizzly autumn morning in late October, a lady from St. Augustine, Florida, came by followed by several from West Palm Beach who were guests of a Brevard family. Shopping in Hendersonville and a visit to the Curb Market were part of their day's agenda. A flurry of activity transpired at the booth, and hand towels plus Dorothy's clever "Microwave 'Baked' Potato Bag" were among the purchases.

I had just finished buying my own colorful "Baked" Potato Bag, considering it a unique discovery. I guess it doesn't take much to get my attention, but since this simple item seemed to promise greater cooking ease, I was intrigued. Directions explain, "This unique bag creates 'perfect' baked potatoes in your microwave. The potatoes will be tasty and fluffy." I couldn't wait to try it out on the sweet potatoes I'd bought for dinner and was more than impressed with the results. The bag worked perfectly, as advertised, quick and simple.

With my selection behind me that morning, I was ready to learn about this family's quarter of a century participation in the Curb. Dorothy's son, Carl Franklin "Frank" Barnwell, was the first to acquire a table at the Market. It was the 1980s, and he and his late first wife, Mary Wilson Barnwell, specialized in braided rugs, chair pads and related items. Both were teachers who appreciated handmade work. According to the "book of memories," Mary was a kindergarten teacher at Dana Elementary before she died from colon cancer. Frank taught at Biltmore Elementary.

"My mother, Mona Phillips Clingenpeel, also got involved at their booth selling baby quilts, stuffed toys and aprons," Dorothy shared. "When I retired from G.E. ten years ago, I came to the Curb fulltime. I have two tables and so does my son. While he no longer does the braided rugs, he embroiders sweatshirts and jackets for children, most of them with the John Deere logo and sayings like 'Git-R-Done' and 'I'm a little Deere.'

"Frank and Mary had two daughters, Anna Marie and Carla. My granddaughter Carla Barnwell Marrow makes Whoopie Pies and sells them here. The Whoopie Pie is a chocolate cake-like cookie filled with gooey sweet stuff similar to icing," Dorothy went on to explain. "The Amish make them."

The history of the Whoopie Pie indeed credits the Amish from Lancaster County, Pennsylvania for the origin of this sweet treat, an experiment with leftover batter that has turned into quite an industry. The "pie" filling is a mixture of shortening, powdered sugar and Marshmallow Fluff, with a touch of vanilla for good measure. Legend has it that both hardworking Amish husband and child alike would shout "Whoopie!" whenever they discovered this dessert in their lunch bags. The pies are considered a *"phenomenon"* in New England, especially Maine, according to the Web site "What's Cooking America." The expressions *"comfort food, weaned on whoopie pies, and a big glass of milk is almost mandatory"* give added insight into what it means to eat one! I hope I'm at the Curb the day Carla brings in a batch.

As the years went by Frank eventually remarried, and his wife Linda Pace Barnwell now contributes to the assortment of clever items gracing Dorothy's table. Linda makes the "Kool-Tie," a specialized tubular neck scarf which offers immediate relief from heat stress, be it from exercise, outside work, or even hot flashes. A good soaking in cold water activates its contents for effective cooling. Now this, too, is worth considering.

Ever the entrepreneur, Frank started Frank's Old Fashioned Ice Cream a number of years ago, a business that enhances both the Curb's "Ol' Timey Day" celebrations as well as other venues. He positions his trailer and sells ice cream made from a Pet Dairy recipe. Last spring I was fortunate to have some, and the verdict…delicious!

As our conversation wound down, Dorothy revealed the secret behind her active Curb Market life. "I'm all the time thinking up something different to make and sell. That keeps my mind active; no boredom. It's nice being here; I enjoy seeing all the people."

With Dorothy's friendly way and satisfying assortment of Market offerings, it's downright delightful seeing her.

Chapter Twenty-Five
A Treasured Heritage
Thomas and Jane Duncan Henderson, and daughter Elizabeth
'Maters, Okra and Purple Hull Peas: True Southern Fare

Catherine and Lindsey Henderson
(Photo courtesy of Elizabeth Henderson)

"We have a heritage that's difficult to walk away from," confided Elizabeth Henderson. As a current Board of Control member and the daughter of Thomas and Jane Duncan Henderson, a family with deep Curb Market roots, she has unique insight.

The morning we spoke together, Elizabeth was busily tossing homegrown ears of corn onto her truck bed, creating an easy buy for those coming to the

Market. She was also shucking corn to sell at her family's tables inside, laden with produce. "Our heritage is the farm, and it's the Curb Market, too," she explained. "Farming is hard work, and you have to be dedicated if you're going to do it. You can't plant and go off and leave the crops, then hope to come back and harvest. It's the same commitment here."

Thomas Henderson
(Photo courtesy of Elizabeth Henderson)

The Henderson family's Curb Market connection goes back to the beginning. The newspaper photograph taken when the Curb opened on Main Street includes Thomas' Aunt Daisy Henderson Pace. Daisy was one of Joanna Arledge Henderson's three children who became vendors at the Market: daughter Daisy and husband Clarence, son Roynald and his wife Mary Morgan Henderson, and son Lindsey and his wife Catherine Frazier Henderson.

Thomas is Lindsey and Catherine's son, and his recollections make clear what the Curb has meant to families. His simple account carries the depth of mankind's ability to pick up and start over, survive and succeed again.

"The Curb Market kept us alive while we were kids growing up," Thomas stated flatly. "My parents were from Silver Creek in Polk County, the lower part of Green River Cove. They came up here in 1917 because of the flood that washed away their saw mill in 1916. It rained 22 inches in 24 hours, and nothing was ever found of their mill.

"It's all about learning to survive, self-survival," he proclaimed. "Daddy farmed and Mother sold at the Curb Market. We were brought up to work hard every day. I'm head strong, hard-headed; you can't sway me from the way I was raised. I've cut back some, now that I'm 70, so I only work 12 to 14 hours a day instead of 16. I farm 100 acres instead of 200. What I do keeps my mind and body busy, and that keeps me healthy, that and eating a little grease every day from the hogs I've cured. I make sure I have my salt, too, because without it I wouldn't last long working in the hot fields of summer. We started a meat processing plant 35 years ago, and we go at it from fall through April. Farming is what I've done all my life. I don't get a financial report, but my wife pays the bills and says we do OK."

Elizabeth laughed when she described her dad and his one-of-a-kind personality; she knew I'd enjoy talking with him. I did! Her love and respect for her father were obvious, though, as she added, "We call our dad 'The Master Farmer,' because he has more knowledge about the how and why of farming than anyone I know. We're taking notes on how he does things on the farm, because once the knowledge is gone, it's gone. This is my parent's life, always has been, and they have no plans to retire. They wouldn't know what to do if they did!

"Daddy's the backbone; we couldn't do this without him. He plants fields of corn, beans and purple hull peas," Elizabeth continued; her straightforward description of her family's commitment to farming a fascinating story, especially for this city girl with Kansas farm roots. "Mom and I plant a large garden with onions, beets, okra, tomatoes, cucumbers, greens, squash, that kind of thing. I grew up working hard on the farm, and that's all Dad knows; Mom, too, since they married."

Jane Henderson
(Photo courtesy of Elizabeth Henderson)

As a teen, Elizabeth would drive her Grandmother Catherine to the Curb on Saturdays and throughout the summers. Later, she inherited her own table from her Great Uncle Roynald, along with the responsibility that comes with it. "We don't really know how to relax, especially during the season. We go six days a week from May through to November. During the day I'm at the Eaton Corporation in Arden, but after work I come to the farm, and my mom and I start picking, cleaning and preparing the food for Market. I enjoy spending time with her; it's something we do together, a connection I treasure that's the most important part of being here," Elizabeth explained thoughtfully.

Her mother, Jane Duncan, was born and raised on Tracy Grove Road; Thomas Henderson lived a quarter mile away. A teacher arranged an unexpected encounter between them and the rest is history, as the saying goes. Their 50th wedding anniversary in August, 2009, featured a surprise "shotgun wedding" and the renewal of vows before family and friends who joined them in celebration at Bethel Wesleyan Church.

"I always said I'd never marry a farmer," Jane stated with a smile and a gesture that indicated, 'but here I am.' She shared delightful pictures of the occasion, including her son with a shotgun slung over his shoulder, exclaiming, "We had a wonderful time; it was a total surprise! We got married in '59 and bought our farm in '62. We have three children: Paul, Sheila, and Elizabeth."

It was a Tuesday in early September when I spent the morning with Jane and learned about her family and the surprise wedding. I had looked forward to our time together, and I wasn't disappointed. The bountiful harvest covering her family's four tables signified the success of their summer efforts. The array of vegetables provided a colorful palette that drew a steady stream of regulars and visitors eager to purchase vibrant and healthy food for their day's meal. It was an engaging morning, as I watched this warm and generous woman interact with her customers who seemed to buy handfuls and handfuls of purple hull peas, yellow summer squash, and tomatoes, okra, and corn, and beans, and….well, the food selection seemed endless!

At first, I was clueless about purple hull peas, but I was soon intrigued. I knew about tomatoes, of course, but had only this summer experienced the exquisite perfection of a true *'mater sandwich*, southern style. Arnold Country White is my bread of choice; Duke's Mayonnaise Light covers two of its pieces, and the slice of a homegrown, Curb Market tomato nestles in between. That's all; that's the recipe; give or take the brand names. The 'mater sandwich does more than satisfy the appetite, I discovered; it imparts a contentment that only comes from good eating.

But the peas were another story. I wanted to learn more, especially how to cook them. Jane was explaining the simple recipe when Willie Mae King stopped by and filled a bag to the top with purple hull peas. She was planning on preparing her mess for a meal that day. Before she left, this gracious lady shared a bit of her life and thoughts about this nourishing food.

"I was born an' raised in Marion, Alabama, an' came here in 1948. I have four sons; my youngest is in Ethiopia," Willie Mae said proudly. "I'm cookin' these peas when I get home. You should try 'em; they're very good, a true southern dish."

Willie Mae's recipe includes cooking the shelled peas with a ham hock and bacon drippings. Jane adds bacon instead, the recipe varying some from cook to cook. The peas simmer in seasoned water or chicken broth for a good 45 to 50 minutes. The next night I fixed my own mess of purple hull peas, steamed cabbage (from the fresh head of cabbage Jane kindly gave me), pork tenderloin, and corn bread, and it was absolutely delicious, if I do say so!

After Willie Mae left, Jim Calloway made his twice-a-week, summertime visit to Jane's booth. Jim came to Hendersonville from Winston-Salem 25 years ago and quickly discovered the Curb Market. "This is a supply house for me; I buy most of the stuff in this bin," he stated.

Rita Helton Whaley stopped to buy lots of corn, tomatoes and summer squash. Born and raised in Henderson County, she explained, "My grandmother came over the mountain from Bryson City and settled here. I love coming to the Curb. I'm a regular customer and always look forward to these days." She filled a bag full of fresh yellow squash, and since my husband is a fan of this vegetable, I was curious how she prepares it. Her easy recipe was an instant hit.

Rita's Summer Squash

Slice the squash lengthwise
Dip the pieces in a beaten egg or egg white
Lightly coat the dipped pieces with PANKO (Japanese bread flakes)
Fry in olive oil

I learned so much during my visit with Jane and took home ideas and recipes that were fun to try, and successful to boot. I also came away with an appreciation for her approach. "I've met a lot of people over the years here," Jane allowed. "Some of 'em are happy, some grumpy. If they're down, I try to cheer 'em up."

I left with a hug goodbye and an invitation to stop by their family's meat processing plant out Tracy Grove Road, past Howard Gap. It took over a month to get there, but the wait was worth it to see the Blue Ridge countryside awash with the fullness of autumn. The drive one late October morning was breathtaking. The fields were an expanse of cinnamon, the trees a revelry of color ranging from lemon to gold and scarlet to pomegranate red, with a subtle brush of lime and pine. Perhaps the poetess Edna St. Vincent Millay best describes the heart's response to such splendor in her poem "God's World." Her first line captures the emotion, "O World, I cannot hold thee close enough!" Autumn is a beautiful season in most any part of our country, but autumn in the Blue Ridge embraces the soul with its glory, plain and simple.

I arrived to spend a fascinating hour at the Henderson Processing Company. My tour began with a look inside the cooler, where I saw numerous deer and a couple bear carcasses, one massive and one less so, hanging up to age before becoming the healthy roasts and burgers coveted by the hunters who shot them. It was quite a sight! Thomas and Jane process a full range of meat, with not an idle moment in the day. Their employees are quick and capable, too, sometimes also working the tables at the Curb. Ike Forbes, who is a meat cutter, does both jobs. He's been part of their operation for nearly 17 years and is well-known by the regulars who stop by the Henderson's Curb Market booth.

It was a lively morning at the plant, as Thomas readily shared his 70 years of Western North Carolina wisdom. All the while, his hands and fingers deftly sliced and trimmed with a rhythm born from years of experience. Without a pause, he quipped to a couple of friends who stopped by, "If we're up, we're doing all right."

Thomas' most endearing comment, though, speaks to the essence of this man and his family. It speaks to those who live by faith, a southern gospel theology true everywhere. "Every day I live is a bonus, according to the Good Book."

From beginning to end, that sums up life. Thanks, Thomas.

Chapter Twenty-Six
Log Cabin Woodworks
David Taylor
Noah's Ark and the Nativity Scene

David Taylor
(Photo by Ann Wirtz)

A colorful, cleverly designed Noah's Ark puzzle is the first item I recall buying from the Curb Market. It was made by David Taylor. This was long before writing a book about the Curb ever crossed my mind, long before I'd written one word for the Times-News, and when browsing up and down the aisles was the extent of my Curb involvement. New to Hendersonville, the

Market was a decidedly pleasant place to spend part of a Saturday morning, and that was it.

During one of our early visits here, my late first husband Arie and I happened upon David's booth, prominently situated next to the back entrance. His puzzle immediately caught our attention. The two giraffes, the white doves, the gray elephant and smiling monkey, the green alligator with mouth open wide, the camel with two humps, even a shark and other animals, well, wouldn't a grandchild love playing with this set? A grandmother certainly would, and now that I'm to become one…I'm ready! Apart from that, however, I knew the intricate puzzle would be simply fun to own.

Several years later, once this book was well on its way, learning more about this talented "woodsmith," David's own Curb Market story, was important to me. I visited him one quiet November morning, just before the 2009 "Ol' Timey Christmas" celebration would usher in the year's holy season of worship and giving. Before David arrived, I spent a few minutes studying the many items adorning his booth. He makes a wooden Nativity scene, beautiful in its elegant simplicity; an actual Noah's Ark, impressive in its size and scope; and a circular design with a delightful representation of the Children of the World. His booth even displays the lovely aprons and crocheted pillows which his mother, Edith Pearson Taylor, still makes for the Curb.

I was intrigued not only with the items on display, but by the wood that lends itself to such beauty. David works primarily with cherry, then oak and mahogany, poplar, even wood from the holly tree, so plentiful in the south. His magnificent Noah's Ark is a rich cherry which has been faithfully hand-rubbed after each clear coat and drying period, a repetitive, day-long process. Noah and wife are hand-painted for a colorful touch, and the assorted wooden animals are dipped in oil. It's an exquisite arrangement, one that can be found not only throughout most of our 50 states but also in Europe, Asia and South America. David shipped two sets the week I spoke with him, his customer-base extensive. He explained, "Some stop by the Curb and see the Ark; others see or hear about it through friends. Word of mouth is a big part of my business."

With his father Carl a cabinet maker by trade, David comes by his talent naturally. As a Hendersonville native, he developed his woodworking skills and knowledge from the youngest age by helping his father in his carpentry shop. "I remember when my parents started at the Curb Market. My dad made and sold a lot of items, but he was especially known for his windmills. They loved it here and never missed a day. It was enjoyable for them to be with their friends and meet the people who come through. My mother is now 86, and she's still making things to sell. It gives her something to do."

The Taylor family has a long connection with the Curb, nearly 40 years. Edith contributed a brief memoir to the "book of memories," describing the usual path taken to acquire a permanent booth at the Market, a place she *"enjoyed...very much."* She wrote, *"I started selling at the Curb Market in 1971 with my husband Carl Taylor. We started selling as day sellers. We got a table in 1975. He sold vegetables and woodcrafts that he made. I make aprons and other crafts."* Several years after Carl died in 1984, David received one of their two tables. He became a full-time vendor in 1999, once he retired from an engineering career at G.E.

Although retired professionally, David continues to use his engineering insight, his observant nature a resource for ideas. Ever aware of design and how things work, David's curiosity takes him away from the area and provides a storehouse of images to draw on for his woodworking projects. "I travel the eastern United States looking for ideas," he told me. "I visit a lot of antique stores. I'm always looking at nature or anything manmade, and then I'll usually design a composite of my observations. It's an outlet which keeps my mind active."

His observations are not limited to design, as he shared thoughts about today's Curb Market. "Being here provides a supplemental income for most of us, which has been down some over the past several years due to the economy. The majority of our customers stop by in the summer when visitors are here on vacation, either renting homes or staying at nearby camps. Unfortunately, we don't see too many young people at the Curb. I'm not sure they have an appreciation for what we're doing."

Probably not, but since this community is home to many young people, and home is where we develop an understanding about ourselves, where we come from, and how we fit into this world, seems parents would be wise to bring their children to the Market. After all, experiencing local history and heritage wherever that happens to be deepens community roots and creates memories that shape a lifetime. "Ol Timey Day" celebrations are a natural for this, but with the Curb open year round, stopping by is easy to do. In browsing the aisles, discoveries could turn into hobbies or careers in woodworking, toy making, gardening or flower arranging, painting, sketching, jewelry making, creative sewing, or a number of other inspiring possibilities. Ingenuity can never be overrated, its intrinsic value the heart of success. With the Curb Market all about ingenuity, from start to future, seems the young could grasp an inkling of that for themselves, given the opportunity.

Spending time at the Curb to observe the workmanship and creativity on display should be, for all ages, part of the fabric of life in Henderson

County. There is much to draw our attention in this world, but we can never go wrong when we connect with our heritage. In the end, it's all about family and roots. With two adorable grandchildren, Rylee Greene, eight and a half months old, and Brady DeBrand, three and a half months, David can attest to this!

Chapter Twenty-Seven
A Mother and Daughter
Ida Barnwell Freeman and Liz Freeman Enloe
From Woven Rugs to Woven Baskets

Liz Enloe
(Photo by Ann Wirtz)

Her baskets make a statement. The beautifully woven baskets displayed at Liz Freeman Enloe's booth invite a stop and consideration, as decorating schemes and functional uses come to mind. Their descriptive names create pictures that Liz expanded upon during our conversation one morning in mid-December:

A Jelly Tote Basket ~ "carries two jars of jelly" ~ and makes a nice gift
A Medium Gathering Basket ~ "was taken to the garden" ~ to harvest wholesome food
A Standard Market Basket ~ "was for shopping" ~ and conjures visions of ol' timey ways
A Storage Tray Basket ~ "holds a loaf of bread" ~ and is an attractive way to serve it
An Oval Basket ~ "is nice for muffins or crackers" ~ or biscuits and dinner rolls, too

The baskets are made of reed, some dyed with a textile dye, some sporting an oak handle. Sea grass is twisted and fills in around the top edge, giving a neat and finished look. "This is a hobby for me. I retired from the North Carolina Department of Health and Human Services in 2001 and started selling baskets five years later," Liz shared and added with a smile, "I wanted to make something different to sell. Since I understood over and under, I decided to make baskets."

Liz comes by her inclination naturally, for her mother, Ida Barnwell Freeman, wove rugs for most of her life. Ida, who started at the Curb during the Great Depression, shares a brief summary in the "book of memories." Ida wrote, *"I have been weaving for over 60 years and growing apples about as long. I take my rugs to the Curb Market and have been since 1934. I have been going to the market for many years and enjoy it."*

Ida is featured in a Times-News article from May 5, 1997, written by Nancy Meanix. Ida expands on the livelihood that created opportunities for her family. *"I began weaving when my son, our first child, was a baby. It keeps, you know. You can let it sit while you do the chores. It will be there when you get time. Rainy days are good for finishing those rugs.*

"Years ago, every farm had a loom, to make their own blankets and other necessary things. I began by doing the stringing for one of my neigh-

Ida Freeman
(Photo courtesy of the Curb Market)

bors. She taught me more about it, after I bought my first used loom from an old lady."

Ida was a vendor until 2003, leaving behind a legacy of hard, yet creative work. Liz recalled, "When I was young, my sister and I would go to the home of our Great-Grandmother Creasy Barnwell for the day, while Mom came to the Curb. She sold vegetables and the apples from the orchard off Old Clear Creek Road which was planted by my dad, Walter Freeman. She'd bring in her rugs to sell, while Dad took care of the farm."

According to Liz, rugs were more profitable and in more demand back then. Along with selling them at the Market, her parents packed rugs in wooden boxes, nailed the lids shut and hauled them to the railroad station during the war years to go to department stores in New York and Florida. While rugs were her primary source of income, during part of the Curb's history Ida was able to sell chickens and eggs, too. Liz recalled the box of ice they needed to keep the poultry cold, something required by the Board as the Market went along. Fortunately, it's still permissible for farm fresh eggs to be sold here, and they're available through some of the vendors.

Opportunities often present themselves because of involvement at the Market. "Through word-of-mouth at the Curb," Liz explained, "my mother learned about a piece of property on Chestnut Gap Road that was for sale. My parents were able to scratch up enough money to buy it. This was the first land they ever bought, and it wouldn't have happened without the Curb. Rug money went into buying land, but it also helped send four children to college."

Liz graduated from Duke University, her older brother graduated from North Carolina State University, one sister graduated from UNC-Greensboro and the other one from UNC-Chapel Hill. Can we doubt the feelings of accomplishment and thankfulness in Ida's heart when her children graduated from college? Every rug she sold at the Curb was worth every moment of weariness and sacrifice for the future it gave her family. Meanix wrote in the May 5 article about Ida, *"Back in 1934 when she graduated from high school in Edneyville, people couldn't afford college, she says. 'But I'll tell you that those apples and all those rugs I sold put all our four children through college!'"*

For nearly 70 years, Ida was a fixture at the Curb Market. She took pride in the quality of her rugs and in helping other members of the Curb. Her booth, where Liz sells today, is easy to find. It's the first table in the middle section, on the right as a customer enters the back door.

The first table on the left belongs to Liz's Aunt Gladys Edmonds Barnwell, wife of Ida's brother, Odell Barnwell. Gladys' table is laden with a wide variety of apples, along with fresh apple cider from her family's orchard, Odell

Barnwell & Sons, three miles from town on Highway 64 East. Her booth is a popular stop, as most every visitor to the area wants a bag of North Carolina apples to take home. I've bought several bags from her myself, and her apples are delicious.

The booth next to Gladys belongs to her sister, Louise Edmonds Ledbetter. Louise and her son, Albert, have Ledbetter's Hand Woven Rugs out on Old Clear Creek Road. I was given the empty table on the other side of Louise for my first book signing, so I had the opportunity to meet these two sisters. It was an enjoyable day at the Curb getting to know them.

I came back a month later and purchased a rug from Louise. It has a "Hit & Miss" design from the red, white, and sky-blue cotton woven together. The rug makes a cheery pattern on my laundry room floor. Louise gave me one of their brochures when I first met her, and the description of their rugs is no doubt similar to the rugs made by Ida so many years ago.

Louise wrote, *"Our rugs are made from cotton clippings we get from hosiery mills that make men's cotton socks. We take the clippings (loopers) and hand dye them. They are then sun dried. Then we hand loop the material together and wind it on wooden shuttles to pass back and forth on several 2 harness hand looms.*

"This business has been passed down from generation to generation. 40 years experience." And even longer at this point.

There is nothing like a family business, and supporting the people who put forth their talents and creativity this way is crucial to a community, to America itself. The more we understand and embrace the Curb's heritage and those who make it so memorable, the brighter the Market's future.

Chapter Twenty-Eight
Memories to Share
Kenneth G. Justus
A Family's Legacy

Edna Justus
(Photo courtesy of Imogene Justus Miller)

"I remember my mother putting me in a box under the Curb table. She'd say to me, 'Stay in there until I get you out, and don't make a sound!' That's probably my earliest memory of the Curb Market," Kenneth G. Justus declared one December morning. His sister, Imogene Justus Miller, later added to the memory, recalling how they played under the table as children until Kenneth was old enough to help their father on the farm.

Their parents are Bennie Fate 'Pete' and Edna Cunningham Justus, a family with a Bearwallow Valley heritage in Edneyville dating back to at least the late 1790s. Still in the family is property acquired sometime after 1794, when the Queen of England granted land to gentlemen who sold or granted several hundred acres to John Justus.

While Pete was growing up on the family homestead in Bearwallow Valley, Edna was in Fletcher. Her parents, Ben and Etta Morgan Cunningham, had a farm on Pattys Chapel Road in Fletcher, where they raised vegetables and chickens and hunted rabbits, all of which Etta sold at the Curb Market on King Street.

Before Pete and Edna were married in 1934, Pete was a barber at the CCC (Civilian Conservation Corps) camp in North Mills River, and Edna worked at the American Enka Corporation plant which manufactured rayon in Enka, North Carolina. After they were married, they moved to the home place in Edneyville, which was deeded to them before his father died several years later. At that point, Pete started carpentry work and farming full-time and Edna started weaving on the loom he built for her. Edna's account in the 1999 "book of memories" shows their progression toward the businesses they became known for: weaving and selling apples. Edna wrote, *"In 1934, Mrs. Coston told my husband if he would put the windows in the Curb Market on King Street she would give him a table. I was selling on the corner table there as I am now. We sold live chickens and vegetables. Back then, they also sold fresh cleaned and cut chickens. I sold cakes, vegetables, and apples. I went to weaving and sell rugs and apples now."*

Kenneth Justus
(Photo by Ann Wirtz)

Kenneth was born in 1937, Imogene in 1939. They were raised on the Bearwallow Valley farm where their father grew cabbage, assorted produce and apples. Kenneth's agricultural knowledge and skills led to the start of the Justus Orchards in Fruitland in 1968, a pick-your-own and a ready-to-buy retail apple orchard. Today his wife, Glenda Fortune Justus, and his son, Don, work the farm and the apple stand, while Kenneth maintains the Curb Market booth that once belonged to his mother. He sells woven placemats, rugs, runners and potholders, all of excellent quality and color. I settled on a potholder, "the best you can buy, thick, 100% cotton and easy to wash," Kenneth explained to me. A good ½ inch thick, tightly woven and able to serve, too, as a pad for dishes hot from the oven, it made a satisfying choice for me. His red and white placemats were a hit at Christmas time, as I observed sets being purchased for the holidays.

Color is what catches the eye, and Imogene had a story to share about the colors in her mother's rugs. "We would go to the Francis & Wright Store off 7th Avenue to purchase dye for the loopers. This was a place that sold farm supplies. Mama would purchase the colors she wanted; then every Saturday afternoon she'd build up a wood fire and boil water in the big black pot she kept out in the yard. Once the water was boiling, she'd add the dye, and in a few minutes she'd throw the loopers into the pot and boil them a bit, poking them down with a big stick. Then she'd sprinkle a handful of salt over the loopers to set the color. Mama would use a pitchfork to lift them into a basket to be spread on big screen frames which Daddy made, and they'd dry in the sun. She had ladies who would loop the loopers together into a long rope which I would later wind on a shuttle. Mama taught herself how to weave, and she wove all the time in the two-story cement house Daddy built for her loom. She could do a 2' x 3' rug in 15 minutes."

Before Edna focused solely on her rugs, Imogene remembered the homemade butter her mother churned and sold at the Curb Market, as well as the cakes they baked. "We would shop at the A&P on the corner of 6th Avenue and Main Street using sugar stamps to purchase the sugar we needed," Imogene said. "Mama would carry her pocketbook; she loved pocketbooks and shoes. After she and Daddy were married, she made $1.50 at the Curb Market one day and bought a new purse. Daddy asked her why she spent the money that way, and she said when she carried the pocketbook to church, no one would know there was no money in it!"

Kenneth has his memories, too, as a boy growing up in the mountains of Western North Carolina. He made his own spending money the same way a lot of boys did in those days. He sold rabbits for fifty cents apiece, cleaned and ready to cook for supper. Caught with a rabbit gum, the rabbits made good eating. While the name he used for a rabbit trap was new to me, it's a common Appalachian term, as is "bee gum." The Blackgum tree, a.k.a. Sourgum or the Black Tupelo tree, is often hollow due to its susceptibility to disease. Bees locate their hives in the hollow of these trees or fallen blackgum logs, hence the term bee gum. Hollow logs make perfect traps, especially for a lad who, decades ago, was interested in making some pocket money. If a log wasn't handy, however, four boards nailed together into a rectangular box would suffice. The door of the trap would be rigged to stay open until a rabbit, or some other unsuspecting animal, ventured inside, tripping the trigger and causing the door to shut.

Another popular revenue stream for a boy back then was to hoe the neighbor's corn for ten cents an hour after school. "If you worked two hours a day, five days a week," Kenneth explained, "you'd end up with a dollar to spend in town on Saturday. You could get a hot dog or hamburger, go to a movie and buy popcorn, and still have change left."

Corn has always been a cash crop. Imogene's son David would grow sweet corn for his sister Leca to sell at the Curb, her counter the back of a pickup truck. Kenneth's sons, Don and Dan, would help David pull the corn. This provided some spending money, but mostly it provided some fun. Leca would also work at her Grandmother Edna's booth, learning how to make change and handle money, all without a calculator.

Memories are treasured in this family and add to our understanding of both the Market's heritage and mountain life during the 20th century. Kenneth continued his Curb recollections with an accurate observation, "Unfortunately, people can't get fresh meat here anymore. We had a meat counter where a person who raised hogs or beef cattle could bring their meat in and Dr. Glazner, a veterinarian, would inspect the meat and stamp it with a purple stamp of approval. This lasted until regulations closed the meat counter."

A side note of encouragement: In the fall of 2009, Wells Shealy from Three Arrows Farm and Cattle Company in Flat Rock began selling beef at the Curb Market. He raises All-Natural, grass fed Registered Black Angus Beef on the farm his father, Dr. Fred Shealy Jr., started in 1981. Wells graduated from Hendersonville High School in 2003 and went on to earn a degree in Animal Science and Business at the University of Tennessee. The farm now continues under Wells' ownership. The Curb is an outlet for Three Arrows beef because it has been USDA inspected and is vacuumed sealed and frozen. That's different than the fresh meat Kenneth remembers being sold here, when chickens were often killed the morning of Market day, or cattle and hogs about as soon. But Shealy's approved way provides excellent, local quality meat for today's 21st Century Curb Market.

Kenneth had another ol' timey story in mind about his Great-Uncle Meredith and Aunt Lizzie Rogers Justus. They lived above the Methodist cemetery in Edneyville, where Uncle Meredith was a blacksmith and a horseshoer who "could talk to a horse and get it to do anything." When they wanted to get a ride to the Curb Market, he'd push a wheelbarrow down the hill filled with his fireplace ornaments and other iron items he'd made, and Aunt Lizzie would walk beside him. Imogene added that after they'd sold their wares at the Curb, they'd do errands and walk to the Community Mill on 7th Avenue where Edna would pick them up.

As our conversation came to a close, Kenneth had some final thoughts about the Curb Market. "It's not near what it used to be. I remember on Saturdays you could hardly get through, the aisles were so crowded. We had a big pot bellied stove, and you had to get here early to get a spot to stand by it to keep warm. People kind of rotated in and out. Times have changed since then. The recent economy has hurt us, but we're still here."

While the ol' time ways and days are gone, the ol' time pioneer spirit still survives at the Curb, making it one of the most important businesses in our community. Visiting the Market and supporting the vendors both honors the past and keeps the present strong, and that's something to remember.

Chapter Twenty-Nine
The Nicest People
Thomas B. Corbett
Bringing a Smile to All Who Stop By

Thomas B. Corbett
(Photo by Ann Wirtz)

"Years ago, the Curb Market provided a livelihood for people, not so much today. For me, it's more of a hobby," declared Thomas Barnard Corbett when I stopped to talk with him about his involvement at the Curb. "I like working with wood, and I enjoy coming here because you meet the nicest people."

Thomas is son to Barnard Bee "B. B." and Bonnie Hill Corbett, who were members of the Curb Market for over 45 years. B. B. was named for his father, who was named for General Barnard Bee. According to Civil War Academy. com, *"General Bee was a Confederate army officer who commanded the 3rd*

Brigade of the Army of the Shenandoah during the First Battle of Bull Run. During the battle, he tried to rally his troops by screaming out the famous words 'rally around the Virginians, there stands Jackson like a stone wall.' From that time on, General Thomas J. Jackson of Virginia would be better known as the famous General Stonewall Jackson of the Confederate armed forces. Tragedy struck Bee shortly after he yelled those famous words, as he was wounded (July 21) and died the very next day (July 22, 1861)."

Thomas shared this bit of Civil War history and added, "My granddaddy was born August 4, several weeks after General Bee died. He was named Barnard Bee in the General's honor, but I'm not sure at that point they knew the General had been killed. The only thing granddaddy remembered about the War Between the States is hiding in the attic with the women when Sherman came through. He was four years old and living in the area around Orangeburg, South Carolina."

The Curb Market started 59 years after the War ended. Stories about that devastating period were undoubtedly still fresh. Remarkably, as far along as we are in time, it remains only a couple handshakes back to the mid-19th century when someone was alive and touched directly by the Civil War.

The Corbett family started selling at the Curb Market in 1936, twelve years after it began. Bonnie continued with the Market until her death in1982. Her children carried on the tradition: Thomas and his wife Martha Tuck Corbett, and his sister Mary Corbett Sitton and her husband David. Thomas is still involved, making it 74 years in 2010 since his parents first became vendors at the Curb. The "book of memories" reveals some of their story, *"In the mid 1930s, Bonnie Corbett's husband, B. B., started keeping bees. Because of the abundance of honey, Mrs. W. T. Capps, a neighbor and seller at the market on King Street, invited Bonnie to share her table in order to sell the honey. This was the beginning...After acquiring a table of their own, they began selling gladiolus, zinnias, roses, a few vegetables, rolls, and crafts."*

Thomas has a few memories of his own about the days on King Street, "My mother was a Hill, and I recall talking about sour apples with Joyce Pace's dad, Lee Hill. He told me the way you make sour apples sweet is to slice 'em real thin and put sugar on 'em! Mother had flowers mostly. I would hang around the booth, helping out some. The Curb moved to this location, and after I married, I brought in flowers, too. My wife would dress bears and make puppets that we sold here. Anymore, I make things with wood."

Indeed he does, making clever items that are short on cost but long on humor. Impressed, I added them to my Curb Market memorabilia. I bought something called "Weather Wood," which is a small round wooden disk hanging from a piece of twine. A bit of the accompanying literature reads, *"To use, hang 6 ½" from your house. By observing the following, you should be able to determine the weather. If it is swaying, it is windy. If it is wet, it is raining. If it is yellow, pollen count is high..."* And so the list goes on, bringing a smile…and a sale.

The other item I bought is called an "Ornamental Mosquito House," which is a small bird house hanging from an angled piece of thin green metal wire. Mine has a yellow roof, but there are multiple colors to choose from. The literature says, *"This hand-painted mosquito house will accommodate 47 skinny mosquitoes or 22 fat ones...In addition to housing mosquitoes, other practical uses are: The enhancement of floral arrangements and potted plants."* I positioned my birdhouse amongst the orchids, a spot of sunshine within the foliage.

For a more serious purchase, Thomas offers handmade fishing lures and hiking sticks. He explained, "I make my hiking sticks with a pocket knife and sand paper. They're made out of dogwood, poplar, wild cherry or birch. They're simple." But they're very nice and would be perfect to use, especially on any of the many hiking trails in this area.

As our conversation wound down, Thomas ended it as he began, "This is a hobby with me. I come in on Saturdays to see everybody. Being here you get to meet folks from all over, and you learn this is a small world. The main thing about the Curb is the people."

They are, in fact, the heart and soul of this place, both vendor and customer alike.

Chapter Thirty
An Entrepreneurial Spirit
Linda Lytle Justice and Family
Jellies to Pickles to Salsas – Yum!

Linda and Lawrence Justice
(Photo courtesy of the Curb Market)

"I graduated from high school in June, was married later that month, and got my first table at the Curb Market in July. That was in 1961, and I was 16 years old; we did things early back then," Linda Lytle Justice said with a smile in her voice. She had called from Florida where she lives during the winter months, happy to reminisce about the Curb and her family's involvement here. She is retired from the enterprise she founded, now under three distinct labels: Sugar Shack, Dana Country Foods, and Dana Fancy Foods. All are retail and wholesale operations that sell locally and throughout the state and are in the capable hands of her daughters and nephew, Robin Marshall Pridmore, Cynthia "Cindy" Marshall Jackson, and Bobby Morris.

"I grew up watching my mother, Caroline Saltz Lytle, make jams, jellies, pickles and cakes to sell at the Curb, and I started doing the same," Linda recalled. "I remember baking 100 loaves of bread a week to sell, but I eventually devoted my energies to making items that were non-perishable. My father, Lowell, would bring in garden produce, but he specifically grew raspberries and strawberries for the Market. My grandparents were here from the beginning, John A. and Cornelia Hyder Lytle, and they sold cured meat and country ham from the hogs they raised. Apples, too; apples have always been at the Curb."

A side note: John A. Lytle was the J. A. Lytle who joined with four others to sign the Certificate of Incorporation of the Henderson County Farmers' Mutual Curb Market on January 21, 1933.

All these years later, Linda's Curb Market business still operates from the same table and location she received as a teenager, the north side of the center aisle, across from the manager's desk. It's impossible to miss her offerings, as multiple shelves extend over several tables and are laden with jams, jellies, pickles, relishes, syrups, salsas and sourwood honey so light and clear you can see your fingers through the glass. A perusal of the colorful jelly jars invites a smile, as one can find every kind of popular and unusual jelly from Kudzu Blossom to Blueberries & Brandy to the number one seller, Jalapeno Raspberry Pepper Jelly. A popular recipe for the latter: Spread cream cheese on a favorite cracker and top it with pepper jelly – instant satisfaction!

"The Lord blessed me with the ability to put things together," was Linda's thoughtful explanation for her success. "A couple of the jelly recipes were my mother's, but most of them are my own. Someone would ask me to do a certain flavor or type of jelly, and I'd try my best to make it. I guess I've always felt I could make jelly out of anything!"

Her innate feel for the successful combination of ingredients led her second husband, Lawrence Justice, to fondly call her "Old Mother Smucker." He appreciated her productivity, having grown up at the Curb with his parents, Sidney and Mae Belle Nix Justice. They started on Main Street and were here for over 50 years, raising their 10 children with the help of the Curb Market opportunity.

Lawrence encouraged his wife's culinary gifts and cheered the development of another popular product Linda perfected and began selling in 1989: Cakes Baked in the Jar. "I had a customer who wanted me to try this, but it had never been done before," Linda said. "No one thought it was possible because the water activity within a baked cake can lead to botulism. But Lawrence thought it was a great idea, and I came home one day to find he'd baked a cake in a jar to prove it could be done. He wanted to take it on the boat to have with coffee!"

Months of experimental baking followed, as Linda worked with precise measurements to create a variety of flavorful cakes that would have a low water activity level. When she was ready, Linda took her cakes to Dr. John Rushing in the Department of Food Science at North Carolina State University to be tested for their water content. "We went over to Raleigh," Linda explained, "but I felt Dr. Rushing had his mind made up, since for a hundred years the government hadn't found anyone able to do this. We left after the first day because I didn't want to waste any more time. Once we were home, though, Dr. Rushing called to see why we weren't still in Raleigh. He had the results: Except for one or two, all the cakes tested a low water activity level. I proved it could be done, and I think he was surprised."

How fortunate we are, as her Jar Cakes are absolutely delicious! Her Butter Rum and Lemon cakes are simply amazing. Linda created 23 different varieties, Lawrence is credited with the Black Walnut Cake, and her sister Barbara Lytle Carter baked them to sell. Lawrence believed they could do it, and they did. A pipe fitter by trade, Lawrence was more involved with the business in the latter years, before he died in 2003. He and Linda were married for 20 years. The cakes live on at the Curb Market and make a wonderful purchase, a testimony to both his vision for these cakes and his belief in his wife's ability to make them.

Linda retired several years after Lawrence died, and she split her business into three parts for optimal growth. Robin is in charge of the Sugar Shack, which makes 100 types of jams and jellies; and Cindy is responsible for Dana Country Foods, which makes 15 syrups, and a number of salsas, butters and the jar cakes. Bobby has Dana Fancy Foods, which makes 60 kinds of pickles and relishes. Robin's husband, Steve, is in charge of the warehouse and has started an online business where items can be purchased at www.blueridgejams.com. While Linda has stepped back some from her business, she's still available to assist and answer the questions that arise.

For Robin and Cindy, their lengthy and extensive Curb heritage dates back to Main Street through both the Lytle and the Marshall families. Their great-grandparents are Cummings and Flora Ward Marshall. The "book of memories" offers some insight into this family, *"They grew and sold all sorts of vegetables and fruits. Flora made jams, jellies, pickles and relishes, also made dolls and sold plants. Cummings was on the Board of Directors. He also used to park cars to help people get in and out of the parking lot. The old timers will remember how small the first parking lot was. This was one couple that really enjoyed coming to the market. They both liked to meet and work with people."*

Flora and Cummings had one son, Ivory, who married Belle Jones, daughter of John and Hattie Laughter Jones, all long-time members of the Curb. Ivory and Belle had a daughter, Sue Marshall Ballard, who had a table at the Market, and a son, Jim, who is Robin and Cindy's father.

As 2009 came to a close, I was contemplating time's rapid pace. My thoughts were centered on the Curb, on 85 years of history quickly achieved, and on the unique people now and from the past who are the story here.

With these thoughts in mind, I stopped by the Market on December 31. I came to buy a few items, to chat with the vendors who've become my friends, and to stop by Linda's booth. I was intent on speaking with Ruby Kent, who's in her second year manning the jelly tables. As I picked out two Jar Cakes, Sourwood Honey and jelly, Ruby explained the differences between some of the items I was considering: Conserve has nuts in it; preserves have bigger pieces of fruit; jelly comes from the juice of the berry; and jams have finer fruit. I was grateful to learn these distinctions.

Before I left, we marveled together at how quickly the year went by. Ruby quoted lyrics to a Kenny Chesney hit that summed up our thoughts, *"Don't Blink... a hundred years goes faster than you think."*

Oh and how the Curb Market proves it!

Chapter Thirty-One
A Mountain Story
Christine Williams Jackson
The Land's Provision

Christine Jackson
(Photo by Ann Wirtz)

"My parents lived way up on Sugar Loaf Mountain almost to World's Edge; it was wild up there," Christine Williams Jackson shared one Saturday in mid-January, 2010. "My dad had 250 acres and a dairy farm. I was 10 years old when I started milking three cows every morning before school. I remember when the barn was hit by a single bolt of lightning and burned to the ground. It was full of hay. Daddy got all the animals out, but it was hard getting the horses. It was a total loss, terrible, and we had no money to rebuild it like it was. That pretty much ended the dairy farm."

But it wasn't the end for this capable family. Christine continued, "Mother and Dad were good providers for their nine children, three boys and six girls. We all worked, starting when we were very young. At two or three years old, we'd take water to the field or pull weeds. We'd walk behind someone in the garden and be shown what not to pull. My parents began selling at the Curb in the 1930s, when the Market was still on King Street. Daddy would dig up purple laurel or wild rhododendron to bring in; they were his biggest sellers. He sold spruce pine and hemlock and would go to people's homes to set them out. I remember coming here with Mother; she'd bring a different child each Saturday. We couldn't have made it without the Curb Market."

Christine was born at midnight between the years 1928 and 1929, third child of Amos and Pammie Morris Williams. "My birth certificate states both years," she said with a smile, acknowledging that in the excitement of the moment, this technicality was overlooked.

We were cozy as we chatted about her family, the rain falling lightly outside, a few customers ambling by as we sat behind her booth, comfortable on tall chairs that made settling back easy. Getting to know Christine was delightful, but reminiscing about life over 85 years ago was priceless. Her story touched on her parent's courtship, one worth the retelling.

Amos Williams worked as a logger in the Pisgah National Forest, specifically the Pink Beds area, named for the hundreds of pink flowering rhododendrons which make this a popular picnicking and hiking spot today. Amos met Pammie Elizabeth Morris there.

"Mama was cooking at the logging camp. It was a familiar area because her family lived nearby above the Fish Hatchery. You'd have to go plum up in the balsams to get to their place," Christine recalled. "Daddy was 21 and Mother (whose own mother was a McCall) was 17 in July, 1921, when they walked all the way to Brevard to get married. Afterward, they turned around and walked back that same day, getting home after dark. When he finished working at the camp, they bought a farm on Sugar Loaf Mountain. They were married almost 70 years when Daddy died in 1989. Mama died ten years later; she was 95. They're both buried at the cemetery at Mountain Home Baptist Church, where they were long-time members."

More than once, Christine stressed how well her parents took care of them. Memories of the various jobs that contributed to the family's financial well-being highlighted our conversation. She explained, "Mother took a job cooking for a man who lived down by the creek. He didn't have a wife. She also cooked pies for the famous Salola Inn, which was on top of the mountain, straight up and a couple miles from where we lived. They had riding stables across the road from the inn, so it was like a dude ranch. People came from

Florida to stay there, and writers came to write stories. As kids, we'd pick berries and sell them to the inn, and they'd give us candy in exchange for the wild flowers we'd bring for their tables."

The natural beauty of the land and its inherent bounty provided an income for those living in the mountains of yesteryear. Beauty and bounty still do. "Mother was at the Curb Market for over 60 years," Christine stated. "She brought eggs, vegetables and plants from the farm. Toward the end of her life, I was working at the JP Stevens Mill and would stop by her home after work every Friday night to pick up her items for the Market on Saturday. I'd sell all day and take her the money. Back then, a vendor pretty much sold out what was brought in. I was glad to keep the booth going."

Christine continued, "I'm the only one of her children who has been involved at the Curb Market. I've had my own table for over 30 years. I married Clyde Bruce Jackson when I was 19, and we worked together until he died in 1989, the same year my dad died. We have three daughters and one son, but only our daughter Hazel is a member here. We sold different items through the years. You never know what people are going to buy, so you try things. Right now I make aprons, baby quilts, Amish dolls, dish towels, covered hangars, scarves, and that kind of thing. I grow my own vegetables for homemade soup, which I also sell." I bought a jar of her soup, and it was delicious and warming, perfect to have on a snowy day in the mountains!

Ol' Timey Mountain Doll
(Photo by Ann Wirtz)

Christine makes two other items that found a way into my heart and home. I had been eying her table for some time, my attention drawn to a doll that seems to embody the Appalachian woman who kept hearth and family functioning during the 19th century. This sweet, ol' timey lady is irresistible with her tiny dark eyes and her large, round nose, her soft nylon face framed by dark hair and encircled by lace. A pink apron sporting a red felt apple covers a country blue dress with tiny white polka dots. An edging of white eyelet peeks out around the skirt's hem. I call her my Ol' Timey Mountain Doll, endearing and symbolic of the people who lived in the Blue Ridge Mountains of yesteryear and are kin to Curb Market families.

The other item I purchased is a lovely wreath for the front porch. In addition to pinecones, the wreath is enhanced with walnuts, acorns, pecans, buckeyes, prickly balls from the Sweetgum tree, and a myriad of other natural offerings. It's just what I was looking for.

As mentioned, Christine's daughter, Hazel Jackson Jones, has a booth next to her mother's table at the Market. She's a floral designer with a business called "Flowers by Hazel," specializing in "silk flowers for all occasions." Her seasonal arrangements add to the beauty associated with the Curb, and at Christmas time her talent is on display as she decorates the entire hall with traditional greenery and the old-fashioned plaid ribbons that speak of the season.

I've discovered something since October, 2007, when I first began interviewing and researching the history of the Curb Market: the more I visit here, the more I find. Treasures abound. It takes time to grasp the whole of this place, its story, its people, its variety of choices. It's simply a wonderful place to find the unusual, but it takes some regularity in coming to make it your own.

Chapter Thirty-Two
Knowing the Ones Who Grow Our Food
Williams, Nix, Capps
A Few More Memories

Arie Williams
(Photo courtesy of the Curb Market)

I was standing in line for a sausage biscuit at the Fall "Ol' Timey Days" celebration. Doug Capps was standing behind me and noticed I was busily jotting down my impressions of the music and the crowd. As we chatted about the day's events and I explained I was writing a book about the Curb Market, he informed me, "We have a table here that's been in my wife's family for generations. You'll want to talk with her."

Indeed, and I finally did. Elaine Nix Capps was gracious to take some time over the phone on an icy, snowy Saturday in January when the power was out at their Green River home and for thousands in Henderson County. The Curb joined other businesses in closing for the day.

It may have been wintry outside, but memories have a way of warming the heart as Elaine reminisced about the Market. "My grandmother was Arie Dalton Williams, and she was raised down Highway 64 toward Bat Cave. She was at the Curb for many years and sold fruits and vegetables, but Arie was especially known for her quilts, every stitch sewn by hand, most of them made from scraps. Several of her quilts were even sold to the Carl Sandburg family, but I don't know what's happened to them."

The first time I looked through the "book of memories," her grandmother's unusual name immediately caught my attention. I was intrigued, since my late first husband and my son are named Arie, a family tradition dating back to Holland and continuing in America through Grandfather (and Great Grandfather) Arie Vanderhorst. It was a surprise to me that a woman was given this name, and it was a surprise to Elaine that someone else had it! This made for a fun conversation, where we discovered our pronunciations vary and that neither of us personally knew anyone else by this name. How her grandmother came to be called "Arie," Elaine had no idea.

"After dinner on Sunday afternoons," Elaine recalled, "my brother, sister, and I would have to sit and listen to talk about the family. We thought it was so boring! Now, I wish I'd paid better attention to what was said."

And what adult child doesn't wish the same. All those experiences, memories and explanations are gone with the passing of parents and kin, and I, too, long for those conversations that are impossible to have now.

Arie's daughter Estelle married Fred Nix, Elaine's parents. The "book of memories" identifies them as *"charter members of the Curb Market."* They lived in Edneyville, "a half mile above Arie," Elaine explained. "My parents grew fresh vegetables, which was their main livelihood, along with chickens and hens. They'd kill and dress them for the Market and for the inns and boarding houses in town. They also sold eggs and apples. I remember when I was young picking wild blackberries to sell at the Curb to buy school clothes."

Her father served on the Board of Control during their years at the Market. Fred died in 1968, and Estelle turned to making aprons. She had a good business, and as the "book of memories" states about her, *"Many households have at least one of 'Granny's Aprons.'"* Estelle retired in 1998 when her health began to decline, and her table went to Elaine, who has had it ever since.

Today, Elaine and Doug are at the Curb Market on Saturdays from the last of May or early June until frost sets in and brings the growing season to a close. They sell a wide variety of vegetables from their farm, a fulltime commitment since Doug retired from Duke Power, where he worked for many years at the Oconee Nuclear Power Plant in South Carolina.

The Capps have an impressive list of vegetables to please their many customers. They sell a variety of peas and beans: Black-eyed or Crowder peas, and Lima, Blue Lake, Pole, Greasy, and Half Runner beans. Added to this are okra, cucumbers, a "ton of squash," tomatoes, but not corn, "a lot of others do corn," Doug said. "We get our food ready to sell and packaged while we're at the Curb, so people can see us and know it's fresh from our farm. Elaine makes wonderful Bread and Butter Pickles, and she grows and sells Calla Lilies here."

And so the years continue, generation after generation; changes take place, but the produce at the Curb Market still comes directly from the farms and the gardens of the vendors themselves. It's good to know the source of our food, but even better to know the people who grow it.

Chapter Thirty-Three
Two We Can't Forget
Hoyte Kerr Jones and Hazel Blalock Whittington
Lessons in Commitment and Self-Reliance

Hoyte Jones, "Ol' Timey Days"
(Photo courtesy of the Curb Market)

The first Saturday in June and the last Saturday in September are the designated "Ol' Timey Days" at the Curb Market. Hoyte Kerr Jones and Nancy and Larry Ball are responsible for this celebrated idea. Designed to thank the customers and to promote the Market, "Ol' Timey Days" has been successful from the start. Today it's replete with a country breakfast, a southern-style lunch, music, exhibits, laughter, fun, and the Curb booths inside filled to the brim with homemade or homegrown merchandise from Henderson County residents. It's a definite come-see-and-participate event for tourists and locals alike.

Hoyte was deeply committed to the Curb, and her contribution to the "Ol' Timey Days" idea is an expression of this. But Hoyte was more than a thinker; she was a doer as evidenced by the numerous pictures in the scrapbooks showing her either cooking ham over a wood stove for an Ol' Timey celebration, or slicing biscuits to receive sausage, ham or gravy. For a number of years, those traditional southern biscuits have been made by Louise Orr and Virginia Bishop, who'd "cut them out the ol' timey way, with a tin can cutter, using what we've got," Orr once said.

After numerous Ol' Timey celebrations and a lifetime at the Market, Hoyte's participation came to an end. The retirement party on August 2, 2008 honored Hoyte Jones, Joyce Pace and French Rogers. As manager Elaine Staton said about the three, "Each one has been here for over 50 years. They all did their part to help serve." All three gave selflessly to the Curb. Hoyte was on the Board of Control for many years, serving as both chairman and member. She always worked to raise public awareness and interest in the Market. She brightened her surroundings wherever she was, including Mountain Home Baptist Church in Edneyville, where she served as the church pianist for 55 years. Hoyte was 85 when she passed away on July 25, 2009, after a fulfilling and committed life devoted to her family, her church and to the Curb Market.

Since the Curb experience is best understood from the actual words of those involved, conversations and quotes abound throughout this book. For those who are no longer with us, scrapbooks and the "book of memories" have provided an invaluable, personal response from the past. Hoyte was one who wrote a bit about her life in 1999, allowing her words to live on. *"It seems that I have always been a part of the Curb Market! I came as a child with my mother, Zella* (Lamb) *Kerr. I remember her selling milk, butter, eggs and vegetables in the market when it was on King Street. I went with her to Flynn's Grocery store on 7th Ave. East to trade anything she had not sold for sugar, salt, soda, etc. and perhaps some bananas or a few pieces of penny candy. What a treat!*

"After I grew up and married, I needed some extra income, so I acquired a table and sold homemade cakes, potholders, aprons and any extra fruits and vegetables we had. Later, I branched out into quilts, table linens and other things that are handmade.

"I am still here after 45 years, still enjoying the privilege of selling at the market, and hope it will be in existence for 75 more years. I love the Curb Market, and am thankful for the opportunity to have a spot here with my friends and neighbors."

One of Hoyte's friends was Hazel Blalock Whittington, another vendor and stock holder who was clever, inspirational, and unforgettable. With a vivid personality and a variety of lifetime accomplishments, simply reading about Hazel paints a picture of a pioneer woman, unafraid to tackle the unfamiliar, self-taught, a role-model for the young.

The Henderson County Curb Market

Hazel Whittington
(Photo courtesy of the Curb Market)

A January 12, 1986 article in the Asheville Citizen-Times titled "Living Off The Land…And Loving It," by Mary Ellen Wolcott, gave Hazel an opportunity to share her resourceful lifestyle, patterned after her childhood in Burnsville, Yancey County. *"'Everything you see around here I made or had a hand in it,' said Hazel Whittington as she sat with a visitor in the sunny kitchen of the 100-year-old farmhouse* (the Kimzey home place) *where she and her husband Clyde live on a country road in the Mills River area.*

"… 'The way I grew up, we lived off the land. You made what you had or you'd do without. We lived on a farm, we had plenty of food but maybe not much money, but if I was ever poor, I didn't know it. I'm so rich in everything, especially my natural resources, and I've got a wonderful, close family. Where we live here, I've got just about everything I need. What I didn't have when we bought this place I have now because I planted and set out trees.'"

Hazel's life was updated in a Times-News article written by Jennie Jones Giles and published on July 1, 2002, titled "An outstanding woman." Giles wrote, *"Whittington has recently added another accomplishment to a long list of achievements and awards. The Henderson County Cooperative Extension Service recently recognized her for more than 60 years of service with Extension Homemaker clubs.*

"She received a lifetime achievement award and was made a lifetime

member of Southern Highlands Craft Guild on April 30 at the Folk Arts Center on the Blue Ridge Parkway.

"...She was an Appalachian Mountain crafts demonstrator at the World's Fair in 1982 at Knoxville, Tenn.

"In 1993, she was one of 60 people chosen to make an ornament for the White House Christmas tree. Her split-oak basket filled with pine cones and tied with a yellow cord is now housed with the private White House collection at the Smithsonian Institution.

"She served on the board of the Henderson County Curb Market for more than 20 years and has been a member since the early 1960s."

Educator, leader, a woman with gumption, Hazel said of herself, *"I learned by doing. When I was 10 my grandpa taught me how to make a broom,"* and from there she so honed her skill that one of her brooms won a prize at the Knoxville World's Fair. She has won untold number of ribbons at the Mountain State Fair and has shared her skills and knowledge with many a person, young and old. Her curriculum is extensive, including how to make brooms, baskets, and wreaths, and how to sew, and do fine handwork, cooking, and canning. She taught 4-H groups, Girl Scouts, Boy Scouts, artist-in-residence venues, and Bible school, to name a few! She considers the teaching of others her greatest achievement.

The community lost a most remarkable woman on May 1, 2003, when Hazel died at age 82. Both Hazel and Hoyte are irreplaceable and dearly missed. They will always be remembered for their abundant talents, vision and irrepressible personalities.

Chapter Thirty-Four

In Conclusion
The Clyde and Sarah Maude Ramsey Pace Family

Sarah Maude Pace's Family, 1977 (Photo courtesy of the Curb Market)
L to R: Sarah Maude Pace, P. Edward Pace (Sarah and Clyde's Son and Lillian's husband), Doris Pace Gardner, Debra Wilder Harmon (now Sawyer) holding daughter, Jaime Leigh Harmon

Reluctantly, this endeavor comes to a close, and what a grand adventure it has been! I can only hope for increased awareness and appreciation for not only the history of the Curb Market, but for what it offers today. It is, after all, one of the most important institutions in Henderson County.

People are the Curb Market, past and present. In working together to create a business opportunity that would address their needs and bring benefit to others, the ol' timers made their mark on this community. They did so with dignity and determination. The Curb became a way of life, and that continues.

Much of the Market's historic record is found in several scrapbooks that have been compiled through the years. Lucy Clark Crawford, a registered dietician, wrote a regular column for the Times-News called "To

Lillian McCall Pace's Family, 2006 (Photo courtesy of Debra Sawyer)
L to R: Lillian McCall Pace (seated),
Debra Wilder Sawyer, Doris Pace Gardner, Jaime Leigh Harmon holding daughter, Maddisyn Belle Hubbard

Your Taste," and several of her articles were based on interviews with Curb Market members. These were saved. One that caught my attention was written in 2002, an interview with Lillian McCall Pace and her daughter Doris Pace Gardner, and granddaughter Debra Wilder Sawyer. The article is titled "Passing down traditions." Their reflections on the Market seem to sum up life in general for Curb families, regardless of what is sold.

Crawford wrote, *"Working in the fields and selling at the Curb Market has long been a family affair for Mrs. Pace. She started going there in the mid-'60s to help her in-laws, Sara Maude (sic) and Clyde Pace.*

"...For Mrs. (Lillian) Pace and her family, their lives revolve around the Market. Doris said, 'You are always getting ready for Market or you are there. You're digging, picking, cleaning, shelling, processing the food, or selling it.'

"Doris has four beautiful daughters that grew up in the garden and at the Curb Market, Debra, Kathryn Cregier, Wendy Hassell and Rita Bergstrom. Debra said, 'That is how we made money to buy school clothes. Plus it was a great learning experience. Each of us learned to work with the public, how to make change, and do inventory. We learned to work hard as well as learned ways of life that sustain us.'

"...Now the next generation is tending to the table at the Curb Market... Debra is growing and selling herbs to continue the family tradition. This summer the fifth generation joined the family business. Kalvin Cregier, 6 year-old son of Kathryn, was selling his own cantaloupes. Delicious ones I might add. His Grandma Doris said, 'He's been working in the garden since he could walk. For 2 years he grew and sold sunflowers.'

"Mrs. Pace reminds you to come to the Curb Market...She says, 'It is

amazing to watch people at the grocery store poking those hard tomatoes from somewhere else when they could come down to the market and get great ones.'"

Perhaps the essence of this family can be gleaned from a sentence in the "book of memories," which offers a delightful description of Clyde and Sarah Maude Ramsey Pace. *"She was known as 'The English Pea Woman' and he was known as 'The Sausage Man.'"* What priceless titles and what a priceless heritage the Curb is, as even today this family is still active at the Market with Debra's business, "The Herb Garden," one aspect of their sales. Most of the vendors then and now could share a similar story, demonstrating the Curb Market's remarkable lineage.

That Christmas classic "It's a Wonderful Life" would occasionally come to mind during this endeavor. The concluding scenes of this timeless movie illustrate what Bedford Falls would have been like without main character George Bailey. The community and the people are shown to be noticeably poorer in spirit and opportunity without him, with life-changing tragedy for some. There's a parallel here.

Can we imagine a Henderson County without the Curb Market, or the losses thankfully averted because the Curb was available? Life is forever challenging, but more than one person has stated their family couldn't have survived without the Market. The depth of the Curb's impact on this community can never be fully expressed or understood, but for those who've benefited and lived it, the reality is personal and clear.

Times-News editor and columnist Mead Parce wrote articles for the "Town Topics" section of the paper, and one published on July 24, 1984 is titled "Fitz-Simons, Hollowell would be pleased." He concludes with noteworthy insight:

"Yet, the idea and push to make a market continues some 60 years later. Maybe 40 years from now some researcher will be checking into the records to write a story about the Curb Market. From the Banks of the Oklawaha *will be the source.*

"The Curb Market is still an institution. But so often we forget the reasons for its being. Some 60 years later the reason for being is the same. Old ways are important. They sometimes are better than the new.

"That's the story behind the story of the Curb Market. Two men who strived to make a community better; to bring people together, not tear apart or create confrontation. The story of Frank FitzSimons and Noah Hollowell."

To honor them, as well as each person and family who has been or is still committed to this invaluable place: Let's keep supporting the Curb. See you there!

Chapter Thirty-Five
The "Book of Memories"
A Bridge to the Past

**Members of the Henderson County Curb Market
75 years of memories**

**Stock Holders, Vendors, and Curb Market Names
Identified from the 1999
"Book of Memories"**

Jimmy & Grace Gilbert Albritton Jr.
Effie Justice Allen
Willis & Bea Griffin Allen
Larry & Nancy Justice Ball
Shannon & Robbie Beddingfield Ball
Sue Marshall Ballard
Dorothy Clingenpeel Barnwell
Frank & Mary Wilson Barnwell
Odell & Gladys Edmonds Barnwell
Wayne Barnwell
Furman & Evelyn Bennison
Clifford & Regenia Bishop
Barbara Blackwell
Frank & Jessie Bradbury
Edith Hyder Brigman
Deloress Brooks
Carolyn Brown
William W. & Maude Maxwell Brown
Jeff & RuthEllen Connell Busbee
Chris Cannon
Douglas & Elaine Nix Capps
L.D. & Catherine Capps
Mrs. W.T. Capps
Barbara Lytle Carter
Jimmy & Tava Carter
James Joseph "J.J." & Mamie Lusk Carver
Andrew P. & Ella Jay Hyder Case
Elaine Gosnell Case

Ethel Duncan Case
John & Eva Lee Case
Madolen Case
Mrs. Tom Case
Paul Chandler
Mona Phillips Clingenpeel
Blanche Cole
Barnard Bee "B.B." & Bonnie Hill Corbett
Thomas B. & Martha Tuck Corbett
Dennis & Beth Corn
Elbert & Irene Henderson Corn
Erskin & Jean Lanning Corn
Katie D. Corn
Mallee Henderson Corn
Gladys Coston
Robert L. & Coela Lyda Coston
Robert & Mary Karen Williams Cox
Ersie Griffin Ratliff Davis
Ethel Hyder Davis
Herbert & Eura Coston Hill Davis
John Lee & Evelyn Davis
Lula Hollingsworth Dill
Roy & Marybelle Drake
Louise Henderson Edmundson
Addie Gilbert Edney
Eunice Farmer
Gary & Barbara Farmer
Frank L. FitzSimons

Jerry Frazier
Larry & Betty Frazier
Ruby Stepp Frazier
Ida Barnwell Freeman
Patricia Freeman
Wash & Daily Lyda Freeman
Valdarine Searcy Gasperson
Jack & Ada Rogers Gebe
Lavon Brigman Gilbert
Betty Goforth
Charlie & Pearl Gosnell
Ulysses & Brownie Griffin
Kathleen Pace Hammett
Lawrence & Brenda Harvey
Robert & Janet Haynes
Elizabeth Henderson
Joanna Arledge Henderson
Lindsey & Catherine Frazier Henderson
Mary Henderson
Millie Henderson
Pearl Barnwell Henderson
Roynald & Mary Morgan Henderson
Thomas E. & Jane Duncan Henderson
Elza & Bitha Hill
Grace Hill
Harvey & Louise Jackson Hill
John & Rosa Revis Hill
Leander & Fidelia Osteen Hill
Polk & Lula Hill
Raymond & Eura Coston Hill
Noah Hollowell
Alan & Marilyn Pryor Horne
Matthew & Cindy Hudgins
James Hampton Hyder
Knox & Altha Willis Hyder
Sylvester S. & Verda Rogers Hyder
Clyde & Christine Williams Jackson
Cynthia Marshall Jackson
Dudley & Essie King Jackson
Dovie Louisa Justice Jones
Fate & Rachel Shepherd Jones
Jackie Jones
John & Hattie Laughter Jones
Julius William "Bill" & Mary Staton Jones
Roland & Hoyte Kerr Jones
Thomas Jones
Ben & Nancy Ann Hyder Justice
B.P. & Helen Youngblood Justice
Lawrence & Linda Lytle Justice
Sidney & Mae Belle Nix Justice
Edna Cunningham Justus
Elizabeth Justus
Wells & Freida Justus
Roy & Velma Kerr
Zella Lamb Kerr
Mike Kilpatrick
Ralph & Vanena Kilpatrick
Albert & Dorothy Jackson King
Charles & Gladys Wilson King
Garland & Millicent King
Glover King
Govan & Mintie Case King
Pat & Jody King
Poke & Apantha King
Ralph & Lucy Stepp King
Ruby Jones King
Irene Harris Lance
Daisy Lanning
Eliza Nix Lanning
Pamela Volkert Lewis
Harriet Lunsford
Garland & Eunice Hyder Lyda
John & Pearl Brown Lyda
Ray & Christine Orr Lyda
Russell & Teresa Drake Lyda
Singleton & Ada Owenby Lyda
John A. & Cornelia Hyder Lytle
Lowell & Caroline Saltz Lytle
Pal & Nora Lytle
Ben & Leola Coston Marlowe
Cummings & Flora Ward Marshall
Earl & Mary Marshall
Ivory & Belle Jones Marshall
Jim & Carolyn Marshall
Kenneth & Harriet Parris Maxwell
Mr. & Mrs. W.H. Maxwell
N.A. Melton
Bessie Merrell

The Henderson County Curb Market

Dewy Dalton Merrell
Jimmie Merrell
Barbara A. Moore
Donald & Doris Dill Moore
Gladys Merrell Moore
Robert Lee Morris
Louise Morrison
D.P. & Lela Moss
James & Rena Murphy
Lamonda Gilbert McCraw
Margaret McDaniel
Alfred & Isabelle Nix
Fred & Estelle Williams Nix
John Nix
Ray Nix
Tom & Milda Guice Orr
Lena Brown Owenby
Dale Gosnell Owensby
Carrie D. Pace
Clarence & Daisy Henderson Pace
Clyde & Sarah Maude Ramsey Pace
Ed & Lillian McCall Pace
Herbert & Joyce Hill Pace
Larry & Reisa Pace
Raymond & Daisy Justice Pace
Mrs. Seymour Pace
Viola Hart Jones Pace
Mr. & Mrs. T.E. Parris
Carroll & Katie Lee Pettet
Robin Marshall Pridmore
Bertha Lanning Pryor
Goldie Ruff Pryor
Patsy Lance Pryor
Robert L. Pryor Jr.
Harley & Lexine Merrell Rhodes
Lola Rhodes
Troy Frederick "Freddie" & Phyllis Ruff Rhodes
Eliza Rhymer
Terry Robinson
Vena Case Robinson
French & Barbrea "Bobbi" Hill Rogers
Mattie Rogers
Myrtle Lyda Rogers
Ray Rogers

Wesly & Frances Rogers
Dexter & Geneva Drake Searcy
Jeter & Pauline Marlowe Searcy
Velton A. & Irene Gasperson Searcy
Gene Silver
David & Mary Corbett Sitton
Carrie L. Pace Smith
Arlene Staton
Herbert & Bonnie Mullinax Staton
Jesse & Julia Case Staton
Robert & Lucille Henderson Staton
Stanley & Elaine Duncan Staton
Mildred Stepp
Clara Swann
Carl & Edith Pearson Taylor
David Taylor
Lois Kerr Taylor
C.G. & Pauline Thorton
Dan Volkert
Herbert & Doris Cooke Volkert
Grady & Callie Case Walker
Patricia Walker
Evelyn Wheelon
Jim & Minnie Owenby Whiteside
Clyde & Hazel Blalock Whittington
Amos & Pammie Morris Williams
Arie Dalton Williams
Eunice Laughter Williams
Mrs. Jep Williams
Mrs. S.P. Williamson

How This Book was Accomplished

"Not by might nor by power,
but by My Spirit,"
Says the Lord of Hosts.
Zechariah 4:6
NKJV

Appendix

Articles from The Hendersonville News as they appear in print:

February 8, 1925, Sunday
CURB MARKET COMING
The curb market is agitated again for Henderson county farmers. It had warm agitation two or three years ago but didn't have the agricultural 'pull' connected with it. I predict a 'go over' this time. County Agent Arnold and Home Agent, Miss Everett, will line up their forces and the thing will go over. Farmers and their wives will line up on the movement. When a small group of farmers learn to co-operate to the extent of placing orders for two car loads of orchard material you may take off your hat and watch them go by for they are determined to do things.

February 11, 1925, Wednesday
FARMERS WILL SELL AT CURB
Henderson county farm products are to go direct from the grower to the customer without the customary peddling and knocking on the door from house to house.
The curb market, the later and more approved method, is to be the solution to the problem.
The Farm Bureau elected Frank L. FitzSimons and Mrs. Gallamore secretary-treasurer of the movement last Saturday and the following committees to help work out the details of curb marketing to the advantage of producer, consumer, and the merchant who wants to handle home-grown products.
On rules and regulations: Arthur Coleman and Mrs. S. P. Williamson.
On location: D. P. Moss and Mrs. Arthur Coleman.

March 8, 1925, Sunday
CITY TO DECIDE ON CURB MARKET TUESDAY, MAR. 9
(Tuesday would actually have been March 10.)
City commissioners are believed to look with favor upon the establishment of a curb market. According to a request of county Agent Arnold, the commissioners Thursday evening asked the committees on sanitation and public grounds and buildings to meet with Mr. Arnold and a committee of Henderson county farmers and see what may be done, fixing the conference date for 3 p.m., Tuesday, March 9.
Mr. Arnold said the farmers would want to begin operating the curb May 1, and that the city owned vacant lot adjoining the city hall, he believed, suit-

able for the purpose until such time as the curb grew out of bounds. Two days a week, at first, will be designated as curb days.

March 11, 1925, Wednesday
CITY GIVES SITE TO FARMERS FOR CURB MARKET
Hendersonville's curb market will be opened for business about May 1, permission having been granted the county's farmers to use that part of the city's property next to the walls on the south side of the city hall. The building, however, will be torn down before that time.

County Agent Arnold went before the city commissioners and told them that the farmers wanted the opportunity to sell from a central place, and the commissioners willingly accepted.

Two days during each week will be designated as curb market days.

May 10, 1925, Sunday
Curb Market Opens On Main Street On Saturday, May 16
(This is the only headline without all capital letters.)
Following announcement that the debris on the site of the old city hall property will be entirely cleared within the next few days, County Agent E. F. Arnold held a conference with the curb market committee of the farm bureau this afternoon, and regulations for the market are being completed, and a date set for the completion of the membership in that movement.

May 20, 1925, Wednesday
SATURDAY, MAY 30, WILL MARK OPENING OF CURB MARKET IN THIS CITY; RULES ARE FIXED
Hendersonville housewives will have the first opportunity at curb shopping and the farmers the first at curb marketing on Saturday, May 30. This decision was reached Saturday at a meeting of those interested in curb marketing.

Frank L. FitzSimons and E. F. Arnold reported in detail their findings on the Spartanburg curb market, which has been in successful operation for the past few years. A big day's sales amount to $400. The sale lasts from 7:30 to 9 o'clock. Those marketing there pay a commission of 5 percent on their sales. This goes to defray expenses incident to having a secretary keep the premises clean, post market prices, make change for purchases, etc.

The secretary gets information on market prices. These are posted on a bulletin board and all farmers using the curb market sell according to the bulletin board prices. These are as a rule a little below store prices and a little above house to house sale prices. Each seller is allowed a three foot space on a long table built under a shed, which makes it possible to operate the market regardless of the weather.

Messrs. Arnold and FitzSimons made it clear that the object of the curb market was not to stop house to house peddling but to afford a central market that would enable farmers to dispose of their produce. No efforts will be made to stop peddling.

The Spartanburg curb market is operated on a very harmonious basis. The prices are fixed and the growers do their utmost to present their produce to the buyers in as attractive form as possible. A governing board of three regulates the affairs of the curb market.

At the meeting Saturday, Mr. FitzSimons and Mr. Arnold were asked to select a farmer to assist them in selecting a governing board. The governing board will consist of at least three representatives from the farmers. They will ask for one from the Merchants Association, one from the Chamber of Commerce, one from the city commissioners, and from the Woman's Club to help make regulations for conducting the market in a way that it will prove attractive to the producers as well as the buyers, and objectionable to no one.

May 27, 1925, Wednesday
PLANS COMPLETE FOR OPENING UP THE CURB MARKET
The board of control has been named, practically all arrangements completed, and plans made for parking of visitors and patrons for the curb market which will hold its initial sale Saturday, May 30, beginning at 7:30 a.m.

The market will open for its first sale at the hour stated, promptly, and crisp vegetables, dressed and live poultry, butter and eggs, cake, pie and flowers will be on sale. It is open to all farmers in the county who want to come in and sell their produce in this way.

Chairman F. L. FitzSimons extends, as head of the board of control, an invitation to all housewives of the city to come out and pay the market a visit on the opening day.

A final meeting of the committee will be held tomorrow morning at 9 o'clock to complete plans. These will include the matter of posting prices, marking locations for the purveyors, and other details. Ernest Cevy will provide free of charge the bags which will be used for wrapping the first day's sales.

On the board of control are F. L. FitzSimons, chairman; Mrs. A. F. Coleman, Tracy Grove; Mrs. S. P. Williamson, Mills River; D. P. Moss, Edneyville; Mrs. Earl Marshall, Dana; Mrs. John Redding (sic), Crab Creek (Mrs. John Redden according to Curb Market records).

In addition to these members on the board, the Chamber of Commerce, the Merchants' Association, and the Woman's Club are all asked to appoint representatives to work in cooperation with the new institution.

May 31, 1925, Sunday
CURB MARKET OPENING FEATURED BY MANY HOME-GROWN PRODUCTS

"The opening of your curb market is a distinct credit to those who brought their produce and placed it on sale. I am well pleased to see the good beginning. It will naturally grow until you will have to provide permanent quarters."

Mrs. Joseph Moody of Atlanta, a guest of the Cedars, thus gave expression to an interest in the subject after seeing notice of the opening in the press. Mrs. Moody is enthusiastic about Hendersonville and the mountain territory and said her patronage of the Atlanta curb market which grew from a small thing to a big marketing center, naturally made her want to see the beginning of the curb market in Hendersonville, which she predicted would have wide patronage once its advantages are made generally known.

The initial opening of the curb market in Hendersonville was at 7:30 Saturday morning. The number of produce growers was few but they had a splendid variety of vegetables, poultry products, cakes, peaches, etc.

The county and home agents, Frank L. Fitzsimons, chairman of the curb market committee, and a number of assistants were present to give any information or help possible to prospective purchasers.

A large bulletin board displayed the prices of the products, which ranged in the wholesale range, and a little lower than the retail stores.

The curb market will be open again next Saturday morning at 7:30. It will be conducted two days each week as soon as conditions and the vegetable crops justify more frequent market days.

June 14, 1925, Sunday
AS THE CURB MARKET APPEARS (photograph)

The above picture shows the Hendersonville curb market on its first opening two weeks ago. The two Saturdays since the opening have been featured by additional farm supplies and an increased number of customers. Housewives are finding it a desirable place for getting the freshest products at most attractive prices.

August 4, 1925, Tuesday
F. L. FitzSimons (photograph)
Chairman of the curb market committee, who points out that all of the larger American cities have successful curb markets which is one of the most ancient methods of marketing.

August 4, 1925, Tuesday
Believes in Curb Market (photograph)
"We may add to the attractiveness of our homes," declares Mrs. George Wing, Jr. (Frieda Elles Wing), secretary of the curb market committee, who is a strong believer in the value of that institution," (sic) by a visit to the curb market every Tuesday, Thursday and Saturday morning.

"Here we find fresh vegetables, fruits, chickens, eggs, butter, breads, cakes and flowers, for home enjoyment. Many of us appreciate this privilege and note with pleasure the rapid growth of our market.

"Let us encourage farm life in Henderson county (sic) by a visit to this market."

Article from The Times-News:

December 31, 1938, Saturday
CURB MARKET HAS BIG YEAR
Officers Re-elected and Plans Are Laid for New Building
The Farmers Mutual Curb Market members re-elected officers today, made arrangements to raze the building and erect a new one on Church Street, and heard a report from the manager that showed a banner year of $28,024.98.

Officers re-elected are: N. A. Melton, president; S. J. Pittillo, secretary-treasurer; Mrs. Robert Coston, manager.

Mrs. J. A. Lytle, Clarence Pace and Mrs. Lila Hill will serve on the board of control with Mrs. Melton and Pittillo.

Calendars

1924

Apr						
S	M	Tu	W	Th	F	S
		1	2	3	4	5
6	7	8	9	10	11	12
13	14	15	16	17	18	19
20	21	22	23	24	25	26
27	28	29	30			

May						
S	M	Tu	W	Th	F	S
				1	2	3
4	5	6	7	8	9	10
11	12	13	14	15	16	17
18	19	20	21	22	23	24
25	26	27	28	29	30	31

Jun						
S	M	Tu	W	Th	F	S
1	2	3	4	5	6	7
8	9	10	11	12	13	14
15	16	17	18	19	20	21
22	23	24	25	26	27	28
29	30					

1925

Jan						
S	M	Tu	W	Th	F	S
				1	2	3
4	5	6	7	8	9	10
11	12	13	14	15	16	17
18	19	20	21	22	23	24
25	26	27	28	29	30	31

Feb						
S	M	Tu	W	Th	F	S
1	2	3	4	5	6	7
8	9	10	11	12	13	14
15	16	17	18	19	20	21
22	23	24	25	26	27	28

Mar						
S	M	Tu	W	Th	F	S
1	2	3	4	5	6	7
8	9	10	11	12	13	14
15	16	17	18	19	20	21
22	23	24	25	26	27	28
29	30	31				

Apr						
S	M	Tu	W	Th	F	S
			1	2	3	4
5	6	7	8	9	10	11
12	13	14	15	16	17	18
19	20	21	22	23	24	25
26	27	28	29	30		

May						
S	M	Tu	W	Th	F	S
					1	2
3	4	5	6	7	8	9
10	11	12	13	14	15	16
17	18	19	20	21	22	23
24	25	26	27	28	29	30

Jun						
S	M	Tu	W	Th	F	S
	1	2	3	4	5	6
7	8	9	10	11	12	13
14	15	16	17	18	19	20
21	22	23	24	25	26	27
28	29	30				

Current and Former Curb Market Stock Holders and/or Vendors

A list of Family Names derived from Curb Market
records, newspaper articles, and
Members of the Henderson County Curb Market 75 years of memories

This is an incomplete list of members and vendors since 1924.
Many families and individuals may be represented by each surname.

Albritton
Allen
Ball
Ballard
Ballenger
Barnwell
Bennison
Bergstrom
Bishop
Blackwell
Boerman
Bradbury
Bradley
Brian
Brigman
Brock
Brooks
Brown
Buford
Burke
Busbee
Byers
Cady
Capps
Caraker
Carter

Carver
Case
Chandler
Chapman
Clingenpeel
Cole
Coleman
Conner
Corbett
Corn
Corner
Coston
Cox
Cregier
Cunningham
Dalton
Davis
Dill
Dolan
Drake
Duncan
Duspiva
Edmunson
Edney
Engen
Enloe

Farmer
Fisher
FitzSimons
Flowers
Frazier
Freeman
Gagnon
Gardner
Garren
Gasperson
Gebe
Gilbert
Gilliam
Gilliand
Goforth
Gosnell
Griffin
Hammett
Harber
Hart
Harvey
Hassell
Haynes
Heatherly
Henderson
Hill

Holbert
Hollifield
Hollingsworth
Horne
Hudgins
Hyder
Jackson
Jenkins
Joiner
Jones
Justice
Justus
Kerr
Kilpatrick
King
Lance
Land
Lanning
Laughter
Ledbetter
Lewis
Liberto
Love
Lunsford
Lyda
Lytle
Marlowe
Marshall
Maxwell
Merrell
Melton
Mintz
Moniz
Moore
Morris
Morrison
Moss
Murphy
McAbee
McCall

McCraw
McDaniel
McMillen
McVay
Nelson
Newman
Nix
Norris
Orr
Owenby
Owensby
Pace
Parris
Pettet
Pierce
Pittillo
Powell
Prestwood
Pridmore
Pryor
Redden
Redick
Reed
Revis
Rhodes
Rhymer
Robinson
Rogers
Ross
Ruff
Sawick
Sawyer
Searcy
Serrano
Shealy
Silver
Sitton
Sivore
Smit
Speight

Staton
Stepp
Summey
Swift
Taylor
Thompson
Thorton
Volkert
Walker
Ward
Warren
Wheelon
White
Whiteside
Whittington
Wilkie
Williams
Williamson
Willis
Youngblood
Zerr

Notes

How This Book Came to Be
   (1) Brubaker, Marvin E. and Eller, Margaret Brubaker. Descendants of John and Anna Myers Brubaker, 1750-1995. Morgantown, PA: Masthof Press, 1996, p. A 13.

Chapter One ~ A Walk Down the Aisles
   (1) FitzSimons, Frank L. From The Banks of The Oklawaha Vol. II. Hendersonville, NC: Golden Glow Publishing Company, 1977, 1998, p. 58

   (2) Ibid., p. 61.

Chapter Two ~ In the Beginning
   (1) FitzSimons, From The Banks of The Oklawaha Vol. II, p. 55.

   (2) Ibid., p. 61.

Chapter Three ~ Pioneer Families
   (1) FitzSimons, From The Banks of The Oklawaha Vol. II, p. 59.

   (2) Ibid., p. 59.

Chapter Four ~ From Under the Umbrellas
   (1) Franklin, Joy. "Curb Market a local fixture," Times-News. Hendersonville, NC, February 22, 1984.

Chapter Five ~ Memories from Golden Glow Farm
   (1) FitzSimons, From The Banks of The Oklawaha Vol. I, II, III, Inside the back jacket cover

   (2) The obituary for Frank L. FitzSimons Sr., dated January 29, 1980, states he served

with the U.S. Marine Corps in World War I. According to Wikipedia: In the civilian leadership structure of the United States military, the Marine Corps is a component of the Department of the Navy, often working closely with the U.S. naval forces for training, transportation and logistic purposes; however, in the military leadership structure the Marine Corps is a separate branch.

Chapter Sixteen ~ A Way of Life
  (1) FitzSimons, From the Banks of the Oklawaha Vol. III, 1979, 1998, p. 154-155.

Chapter Seventeen ~ Lining up for Iris, Peaches, Apples and Plants
  (1) The Encyclopedia of American Food and Drink by John Mariani. New York: Lebhar-Friedman Books, 1999.

Chapter Nineteen ~ Venetian Art Glass and Sourdough Bread
  (1) www.artofvenice.com
  (2) www.venetianglassart.com

More Pictures from the Henderson County Curb Market

Curb Market Vendors, 1974 (Photo by June Glenn Jr., courtesy of the Curb Market)
L to R: Raymond Pace, Hoyte Jones, Hazel Whittington, Verda Hyder,
Arie Williams, Ersie Ratliff Davis, Gladys Coston, Daisy Pace

Vena Robinson, "Ol' Timey Days"
(Photo courtesy of the Curb Market)

Elizabeth Henderson
(Photo courtesy of Elizabeth Henderson)

Governor Bev Perdue (Photo by Ann Wirtz)
L to R: Gladys Barnwell, Bob Eaves, N.C. Governor Beverly Eaves Perdue
The Governor's March 6, 2010 visit to the Curb Market

Pat Lyda Mintz (Photo by Ann Wirtz)

Larry Ball and Pop Rogers, "Ol' Timey Days"
(Photo courtesy of the Curb Market)

Mrs. George Wing Jr. (Frieda Elles Wing), "secretary of the curb market committee, who is a strong believer in the value of that institution." More information on Mrs. Wing is availabe in the Appendix. (Photo courtesy of The Hendersonville News, August 4, 1925)

AJ Moniz (Sandy and Joshua),
Simply Natural Gifts
(Photo by Ann Wirtz)

Lavon Gilbert (Photo by Ann Wirtz)

Wells Shealy, Three Arrows Farm and Cattle Company
(Photo by Ann Wirtz)

Ellen McMillen, Cottage Creations
(Photo by Ann Wirtz)

Janet Gardner, WeLuvGems
(Photo by Ann Wirtz)

Carol Pierce, Carol's Canine Creations
(Photo by Ann Wirtz)

Will Buford (and Tambra), Vineyards Edge Farm
(Photo by Ann Wirtz)

Mary Sivore, Smoky Mountain Soaps and Scents
(Photo by Ann Wirtz)

www.ingramcontent.com/pod-product-compliance
Lightning Source LLC
Chambersburg PA
CBHW052030070526
44584CB00016B/1972